YORK NOTES

THE WHITE DEVIL

JOHN WEBSTER

NOTES BY JAN SEWELL

Longman

York Press

The right of Jan Sewell to be identified as Author of this Work has been asserted by her in accordance with the Copyright, Designs and Patents Act 1988

YORK PRESS
322 Old Brompton Road, London SW5 9JH

PEARSON EDUCATION LIMITED
Edinburgh Gate, Harlow,
Essex CM20 2JE, United Kingdom
Associated companies, branches and representatives throughout the world

Quotations from *The White Devil* by John Webster are from the New Mermaids edition of the play edited by Christina Luckyi and published by Methuen Drama, an imprint of A & C Black Publishers (second edition 1996, 2006)

10 9 8 7 6 5 4

ISBN 978–1–4058–9621–4

Phototypeset by Pantek Arts Ltd, Maidstone, Kent
Printed in China (EPC/04)

CONTENTS

PART ONE

INTRODUCTION

STUDYING PLAYS

Reading plays and exploring them critically can be approached in a number of ways, but when reading the text for the first time it is a good idea to consider some, or all, of the following:

- **Format and style**: how do plays differ from other genres of text? How are scenes or acts used to reveal information, and how do the characters convey their emotions?

- **The writer's perspective**: consider what the writer has to say, how he or she presents a particular view of people, the world, society, ideas, issues, etc. Are, or were, these views controversial?

- **Shape and structure**: explore the relationship between scenes and acts, plots and sub-plots, and how the action of the play develops – the moments of revelation and reflection, openings and endings, conflicts and resolutions.

- **Choice of language**: does the writer choose to write formally or informally? Does he or she use different registers for characters or groups, vary the sound and style, or employ verse, prose, and other language features such as **imagery** and **dialect**?

- **The play in performance**: how do you imagine the play being performed? What contribution might set design and the actors' voices and movements make?

- **Links and connections**: what other texts does this play remind you of? Can you see connections between its **narrative**, main characters and ideas and those of other texts you have studied? Is the play part of a literary movement or tradition?

- **Your perspective and that of others**: what are your feelings about the play? Can you relate to the characters, themes and ideas? What do others say about the play – for example, critics, other writers, actors and directors?

These York Notes offer an introduction to *The White Devil* and cannot substitute for close reading of the text and the study of secondary sources.

CHECK THE BOOK
The Cambridge Companion to English Renaissance Drama edited by A. R. Braunmuller and Michael Hattaway (Cambridge UP, 2003) is a good introduction and has a useful chapter on 'Tragedy'.

READING *THE WHITE DEVIL*

The White Devil was published in 1612 and first performed at the Red Bull Theatre earlier that year. It is a complex and disturbing play in which private vice, political corruption and sexual intrigue are played out against a public world of splendour and magnificence. The 'White Devil' of the title meant a 'hypocrite' and came from the proverb: 'The white devil is worse than the black'. A number of the characters are candidates for the role in Webster's play, although one critic argues that it 'stands not for one of the *dramatis personae*, or even several of them, but for a certain moral attitude, a scheme of values' (Anders Dallby, *The Anatomy of Evil: A Study of John Webster's The White Devil*, CWK Gleerup Lund, 1974, p. 38). The play depicts the seduction of the beautiful, married, Vittoria Corombona by the powerful Duke of Brachiano. The consummation of their relationship leads to murder, madness, a trial, excommunication, flight and a wedding, and initiates a series of bloody revenges.

Set in Renaissance Italy, the themes the play explores were just as relevant to the Jacobean court of John Webster's native London. Up to this point most of Webster's plays had been collaborative works written with a number of fellow-playwrights. He continued to write plays throughout his life including the **tragicomedy** *The Devil's Lawcase* as well as celebrations of London in civic pageants such as the Merchant Taylors' *Monuments of Honour* (1624). Today, however, Webster is mainly remembered and admired for his two great **tragedies**, *The White Devil* (1612) and *The Duchess of Malfi* (published 1623; written and first performed 1613–14).

T. S. Eliot famously wrote, 'Webster was much possessed by death / And saw the skull beneath the skin' ('Whispers of Immortality', from *Poems*, 1920). This is a comment on the tragic quality of his vision in plays which explore the dark underside of contemporary life. *The White Devil* examines the workings of power and corruption. Webster explores the options for ambitious individuals in a social order which is breaking down but still based on the power of a feudal aristocracy and the Church, and considers the role of women in a **patriarchal** society in which they are seen as naturally subservient to men. The play questions the extent to

CONTEXT

Renaissance means 'rebirth' and describes a cultural movement from the fourteenth to the seventeenth centuries, which started in Italy in the late middle ages and spread throughout the rest of Europe. It was characterised by a renewed interest in the classical writings of ancient Greece and Rome, educational reform and the development of perspective in art.

CONTEXT

'Elizabethan' describes the period from 1558–1603, whereas 'Jacobean' describes the rule of James I of England (1603–25) – from *Jacobus* (Latin for James). James was also James VI of Scotland.

which the fates of individual characters are determined by their own free will, by social structures and forces, by the vagaries of chance and a capricious fortune, or by the workings of divine providence.

The White Devil is generally classified as **revenge tragedy**, a genre with which the play shares many characteristics although revenge is not the main plot element – certainly not in the first half. Revenge tragedy typically dramatises characters who take justice into their own hands to avenge a crime despite the biblical injunction against it. Such plays show the corrupting effect of an ensuing cycle of violence which finally spirals out of control and inevitably leads to the deaths of all the main protagonists. The genre was much influenced by the tragedies of the Roman playwright, Seneca. Thomas Kyd's *The Spanish Tragedy*, written in the late 1580s, is the first example on the English stage. It was immediately popular and created a new dramatic genre which included plays such as Thomas Middleton's *The Revenger's Tragedy*, John Marston's *The Malcontent* (with additions by Webster) and *Antonio's Revenge*, Cyril Tourneur's *The Atheist's Tragedy* and the most famous example, Shakespeare's *Hamlet*. Revenge drama is often self-conscious and contains moments of black humour and self-parody, what Nicholas Brooke called *Horrid Laughter in Jacobean Tragedy* (Open Books, 1979). Characters in revenge tragedy typically make witty, **satirical** comments, and the sensational events onstage often strike the audience as bizarre, ludicrous and over the top.

Despite an initial failure to please – see Webster's address 'To the Reader' (p. 5) in which he explains this in terms of the weather and the unsuitability of the Red Bull as a venue which generally catered for a lower class, poorly educated audience, unable to appreciate the subtlety and sophistication of his play – *The White Devil* went on to enjoy later success. It was revived in 1630 by Queen Henrietta's Men at the Phoenix theatre in Drury Lane and the text reprinted three times in the seventeenth century. It is now regarded as one of the greatest plays in the period, offering a complex tragic vision of a morally corrupt society.

The White Devil, although written nearly two hundred years before the **gothic** as a genre became well defined, like many earlier works has an obvious affinity with the later genre. Gothic fiction is usually

CONTEXT

Revenge drama was popular on the Elizabethan and Jacobean stage, partly due to the influence of the Roman playwright Seneca and partly on account of its contemporary relevance to a society in which the rule of law was not yet established. Revenge is prohibited in the Bible: 'Dearly beloved, avenge not yourselves, but rather give place unto wrath: for it is written, Vengeance is mine; I will repay, saith the Lord' (Romans 12:19).

 CHECK THE BOOK

The Revenger's Tragedy (1607) is, as its title implies, a classic example of revenge tragedy and exhibits all the characteristics of the genre. Scholars used to credit authorship to Cyril Tourneur but most are agreed nowadays that it was almost certainly by Webster's friend and collaborator Thomas Middleton.

associated with a literary genre which has its roots in novels of the eighteenth century such as Horace Walpole's *The Castle of Otranto* (1764) and Ann Radcliffe's *The Mysteries of Udolpho* (1794). The typical features of **gothic** fiction are horror, romance, mystery, supernatural elements such as ghosts, gothic architecture (in practice this tends to mean medieval castles with winding corridors), **melodrama**, and a fascination with death, darkness and decay. Gothic texts also often contain comic elements including a tendency to self-conscious **parody** and exaggeration. *The White Devil* shares many features of the later genre including an apparently rambling, episodic structure, a fascination with death and corruption, and a tendency towards the macabre and shocking.

In many ways *The White Devil* seems a modern play in its sharpness of observation, cynicism, **irony** and self-conscious questioning. The writing has an edginess which resonates with the anxieties of contemporary western culture. The characters are ambiguous and hard to know or like. The central characters, Flamineo and Vittoria, appear the most attractive and the audience are likely to identify with their liveliness, intelligence and courage despite, or perhaps because of, recognising that there is something dangerous and desperate about them. Studying the play today offers the modern reader an understanding of the social anxieties, pressures and conflicts which characterised Renaissance drama and the early modern period. It also helps us understand the way in which drama works, how our peculiar cultural fascination with certain elements, notably sex and death, are deployed to signify wider social questions. Sex is constantly emphasised and becomes a sort of surrogate for politics (generally regarded as dull and non-dramatic). The play continues to challenge audiences and readers with the question of how to live life in a fragile world in which nothing seems certain. It asks searching questions about ambition, moral compromise and the problem of evil without offering facile answers or easy social solutions. For this reason it continues to fascinate and disturb. It is ultimately for the modern audience or readers to confront the dilemmas the play dramatises and tease out their own meaning and solutions to the issues it explores.

> **CONTEXT**
>
> The early modern period is the period from the late middle ages to the industrial revolution – roughly 1500–1800.

PART TWO

THE TEXT

NOTE ON THE TEXT

The White Devil was first printed in 1612 by Nicholas Okes in a quarto text. Okes was well known as a printer of English Renaissance plays who had served his apprenticeship with Richard Field, Shakespeare's friend and fellow-Stratfordian. The play was probably printed from Webster's 'foul papers', and contains his address 'To the Reader' in which Webster justifies publication and defends the play's recent unsuccessful production. Three further seventeenth-century editions were based on this. Apart from Nahum Tate's adaptation of 1707, *Injured Love: or, The Cruel Husband*, the play has not undergone subsequent revision. In the twentieth century renewed interest has resulted in various modern editions, notably F. L. Lucas's *The Complete Works of John Webster* (1927, Chatto and Windus, republished 1966), Elizabeth Brennan's earlier New Mermaid's edition (1966), John Russell Brown's *The Revels Plays* (Manchester University Press, second edition, 1966), and Gamini Salgado in *Three Jacobean Tragedies*, (The Penguin English Library, 1965). The edition used in preparation of these Notes is the New Mermaid's edition (2006), edited by Christina Luckyj.

SYNOPSIS

The play is set in Rome and opens with an Italian nobleman, Count Lodovico, complaining to his friends Gasparo and Antonelli that he has been banished from the city for his dissolute behaviour and crimes of murder. He complains that the Duke of Brachiano has not suffered a similar punishment. Gasparo and Antonelli attempt to offer comfort and reconcile him to his fate but he vows to revenge himself on his enemies.

The Duke of Brachiano starts a sexual liaison with a beautiful married woman, Vittoria Corombona. Brachiano's affair with Vittoria is contrived by his personal secretary, Flamineo, who is also

CONTEXT

A quarto was a small, cheap paperback edition of a play. Plays belonged to the acting company for which they were written, so authors did not earn money from their publication and were not always mentioned on the title page.

CONTEXT

The term 'foul papers' refers to a playwright's working draft of a play. A 'fair copy' would normally be made by the playwright or a professional scribe to be annotated for use as an acting company 'book'. 'Foul papers' can sometimes reveal evidence of an author's first thoughts or mistakes.

Vittoria's brother. Vittoria tells Brachiano about a macabre dream she has had of the deaths of her husband, Camillo, and Brachiano's wife, Isabella. Vittoria's mother, Cornelia, accuses Vittoria and Brachiano of adultery and tells Brachiano that his wife, the duchess Isabella, has arrived in Rome.

Francisco de Medici, Isabella's brother, and Cardinal Monticelso, Camillo's uncle, complain to Brachiano about his relationship with Vittoria. Francisco tries to reconcile Brachiano with Isabella, but Brachiano cruelly rejects his wife and she returns to Padua. Flamineo, however, has already arranged for the duchess to be poisoned by a doctor, Julio, and plans to take care of his brother-in-law Camillo's death personally.

Lodovico (also known as Lodowick) has meanwhile become a pirate and Camillo is appointed to capture him, with the help of Vittoria and Flamineo's brother, Marcello. Monticelso and Francisco (Camillo's uncle and Isabella's brother respectively) warn Camillo of Vittoria's infidelity. They believe that Camillo has been deliberately appointed in order to get him out of the way so that the duke, Brachiano, can have access to Vittoria. They hope that Brachiano will be involved in a public scandal and disgraced. Count Lodovico meanwhile goes to Padua to ask Isabella, whom he loves, to secure his pardon.

A conjuror shows Brachiano two **dumb shows**; in the first Doctor Julio applies poison to Brachiano's portrait which Isabella then kisses and dies. The second shows Camillo's death in the midst of celebrations for his forthcoming journey when Flamineo 'accidentally' breaks his brother-in-law's neck on a vaulting-horse.

Vittoria and her brothers, Flamineo and Marcello, are arrested for her husband's murder. Vittoria is arraigned, that is brought before a tribunal presided over by Monticelso, accused both of Camillo's murder and of immoral behaviour. Vittoria defends herself in a spirited manner. Due to lack of evidence concerning Camillo's death, Vittoria's brothers Marcello and Flamineo are discharged but Vittoria is publicly disgraced and sent, with her Moorish maid Zanche, to a house of convertites or 'penitent whores'. Brachiano returns to the court to make friends with his brother-in-law

> **CONTEXT**
>
> Despite Elizabeth I's unsuccessful attempts to expel them in 1596 and 1601, 'blackamoors' were an everyday sight in London and became fashionable as servants to the rich, supposedly because their colour emphasised the whiteness of their employers' skin.

Francisco. Brachiano and Isabella's son Giovanni arrives with Count Lodovico and tells his uncle, Francisco, and the cardinal of the duchess's death.

Embittered by the lack of reward for his services to Brachiano, Flamineo forms a pact with Lodovico and they bemoan their misfortunes. Lodovico then learns that Francisco has interceded on his behalf with the dying Pope who has granted his pardon. Flamineo is furious and he and Lodovico argue and fight.

Isabella's brother, Francisco, and Cardinal Monticelso discuss avenging her death. Francisco favours secrecy rather than open warfare. He takes the cardinal's 'black book' which records the names of villains and their crimes. Isabella's ghost appears to him. Hoping to incite Brachiano's jealousy and draw him into a trap, Francisco writes Vittoria a love-poem in which he claims he will take her away and set her free from her imprisonment. He decides to employ Lodovico to help him execute his vengeance.

Flamineo and Brachiano visit Vittoria in the house of convertites. Brachiano intercepts Francisco's poem, is overcome with jealousy and accuses Vittoria of infidelity. She is furious with Brachiano and Flamineo, and defends herself against them both. They are chastened and, as Francisco had planned, inspired by his poem, Brachiano decides to rescue Vittoria, take her away with him to Padua and marry her.

A conclave is held to choose the next Pope. Francisco learns that Vittoria has fled with Brachiano. Cardinal Monticelso is elected Pope and his first papal act is to excommunicate Brachiano and Vittoria. Francisco reminds Lodovico that he has sworn to murder Brachiano. Monticelso is curious about Francisco's motive for urging Lodovico's pardon. In a **parody** of the Catholic sacrament of confession Lodovico says that he loved Isabella and has sworn to avenge her murder – making him the perfect tool for Francisco's revenge. Monticelso warns Lodovico that he will be damned eternally and Lodovico decides not to continue. Francisco, however, sends a servant to Lodovico with a thousand ducats pretending they are from the Pope and Lodovico changes his mind again.

> **CONTEXT**
>
> A 'convertite' was most commonly used to refer to someone who had converted to a religious faith or way of life but also meant 'a reformed Magdalen', that is, a reformed prostitute named after Mary Magdalen in the Bible.

> **CONTEXT**
>
> England was a Protestant rather than a Catholic country when Webster was writing. Following the divorce of Henry VIII from Katherine of Aragon, Henry had declared himself head of the Church by the 1534 Act of Supremacy. He then seized and took control of land owned by the Church through the dissolution of the monasteries.

CHECK THE BOOK

The corruption of the Catholic Church was a frequent theme of English Renaissance drama. See, for example, the portrait of the wily Cardinal Pandulph in Shakespeare's *King John*.

Brachiano and Vittoria are married and Flamineo believes that his luck has finally changed. However Francisco, Lodovico, Antonelli, and Gasparo with others of his men, have disguised themselves and joined Brachiano's court as a Moor and Capuchin monks. They plan to poison Brachiano.

Cornelia and Marcello, also at court, object to Vittoria's maid Zanche and her relationship with Flamineo. Cornelia strikes her and Marcello kicks her. Angered by their treatment, Flamineo challenges his brother, Marcello, to a duel. Zanche meanwhile tells Francisco, disguised as the Moor, Mulinassar, that she loves him and that she can tell him many secrets. Flamineo kills his brother Marcello. Cornelia tries to avenge his death but cannot and, fearful of losing her only remaining son, defends Flamineo, telling Brachiano that the death of Marcello was an accident.

Before the tournament to celebrate Vittoria and Brachiano's wedding, Lodovico sprinkles the mouthpiece of Brachiano's helmet with poison. The tournament begins and the men fight; the poison takes effect. Brachiano knows he is going to die and starts to lose his wits. He is eventually strangled by the disguised monks after they reveal their true identities to the dying duke and confront him with his sins. Vittoria is distraught. Zanche suggests an elopement with the disguised Francisco and tells him how Isabella and Camillo were both murdered.

Brachiano's son, Giovanni, the new young duke, overhears Flamineo making insulting remarks about him and forbids his presence. Cornelia goes mad and performs Marcello's funeral rites. Brachiano's ghost appears to Flamineo.

Lodovico tells Francisco he should leave the city now otherwise he won't carry out Vittoria's murder. Hortensio, one of Brachiano's officers, overhears them and goes to raise a force to prevent further violence. Flamineo demands to know how his sister, who has been made Brachiano's heir, will repay him for his loyal service to the duke. She accuses him of Marcello's murder and refuses to give him anything. He threatens her with pistols and claims that Brachiano had given orders that neither of them should outlive him. Vittoria and Zanche try to trick Flamineo by shooting him first and believe they have killed him but he jumps up and tells them the guns were not loaded.

Lodovico and Gasparo enter and reveal their true identities. They kill Zanche, Vittoria and Flamineo in turn. Vittoria dies bravely but ultimately penitent. Flamineo is defiant to the end. Giovanni and the guards arrive and shoot at the conspirators, Lodovico and Gasparo. Lodovico tells Giovanni that they were hired by his uncle, Francisco, who was also the Moor in disguise and responsible for Brachiano's death. Giovanni orders the removal of the bodies and those remaining onstage to consider their own moral failings.

DETAILED SUMMARIES

ACT I

SCENE 1

- Count Lodovico reveals he has been banished.
- His friends, Antonelli and Gasparo, attempt to comfort him.

As the scene opens we learn that Count Lodovico has been banished from Rome. He complains that the sentence is unjust and blames it on powerful enemies, but Antonelli and Gasparo suggest that his dissolute and violent behaviour has merited the punishment and attempt to reconcile him to his fate. He dismisses the murders he has committed as mere 'flea-bitings' (line 33), rejects their advice, 'Leave your painted comforts' and promises to be revenged in future, 'I'll make Italian cut-works in their guts / If ever I return' (lines 50–2). He is bitter that the Duke of Brachiano has not suffered similar punishment for his crimes, and complains that Vittoria Corombona might have 'got my pardon / For one kiss to the Duke' (lines 43–4).

QUESTION

The White Devil has been frequently criticised for the 'rambling', 'loose', **'gothic'** nature of its plot. What is your impression from the synopsis given?

CONTEXT

Banishment was a contemporary punishment for noblemen who have committed a crime; it was dramatised in a number of plays in the period including Shakespeare's *Richard II*, when Henry Bolingbroke and Thomas Mowbray are banished and *Romeo and Juliet* when Romeo accidentally kills Tybalt and is banished from Verona.

SCENE 1 continued

CONTEXT

Fortune was frequently **personified** as the Roman goddess Fortuna who spun her wheel at random causing sudden reversals in luck – some people were rewarded without merit while others suffered undeserved misfortune. In III.3.95 Flamineo associates 'Fortune's wheel' with an instrument of torture.

COMMENTARY

The effect of the opening line, Lodovico's 'Banished?' is abrupt and dramatic. In this short opening scene Webster introduces themes which are central to the play through characters who, at first sight, seem peripheral. Count Lodovico is angry and unrepentant, blaming his banishment on an unjust 'Fortune' (line 4) – and the machinations of powerful enemies. This touches on the play's central concerns: corruption of the law and its abuse by the rich and powerful. As Lodovico puts it, 'Your wolf no longer seems to be a wolf / Than when she's hungry' (lines 8–9) – a wealthy man is not considered a criminal in the way a poor, needy one is. It also raises questions about the extent to which anyone is responsible for his or her own fate, whether bad luck can be simply blamed on malevolent 'Fortune', or the enmity of the powerful.

GLOSSARY

3	**Democritus** Greek philosopher of the fifth century BC, who believed that reward and punishment governed the world
7	**quite** requite, repay
12	**pashed** dashed
16	**mummia** medicine originally prepared from mummified flesh
18	**kennel** gutter
19–21	**One citizen … caviar** a citizen, i.e. one of lower social class but richer than Lodovico, flattered him, calling him 'master' in order to obtain caviar, a rare luxury
22	**prodigal** wasteful, extravagant
29–30	**This … either** Lodovico complains that the alternate sayings of his two friends are like two buckets drawing up mechanical comforts in turn from a common well
31	**acted** committed
36	**gentle penance** easy sentence appropriate to a nobleman
41	**close panderism** secret attempts to gratify his lust
44	**Have a full man within you** be a proper complete man
47	**chafed** heated, rubbed
50	**painted** false, artificial
51	**Italian cut-works** openwork embroidery

CONTEXT

The 'phoenix' (line 23) is a mythical Arabian bird which was unique and lived for five to six hundred years; a new one was born from its ashes; the implication is that Lodovico's feasts were so greedy and extravagant that they were almost prepared to eat even this rare creature.

SCENE 2

- Brachiano confides his passion for Vittoria to his secretary, her brother Flamineo.
- Flamineo reassures Brachiano that he will arrange a meeting and tricks her husband, Camillo, into sleeping alone.
- Brachiano and Vittoria lie down together and she relates her dream of the deaths of her husband and his wife.
- Cornelia, Vittoria and Flamineo's mother, interrupts the lovers, accuses them of adultery and tells the duke that the duchess has arrived in Rome.
- Brachiano leaves. Flamineo blames his mother for upsetting the duke and for the poverty which he claims is the cause of his and Vittoria's behaviour.

Brachiano and Flamineo have been visiting Camillo and Vittoria. When it is time to retire for the night Brachiano prepares to leave, despairing of seeing Vittoria alone, telling Flamineo he is 'Quite lost' (line 3). Flamineo reassures him that he will contrive a meeting between them – he has already engaged the help of Vittoria's servant Zanche – and tells the duke to hide in a cupboard, while warning him against his passion, 'I must not have your lordship thus unwisely amorous' (line 39). Camillo meanwhile confides to Flamineo that he and Vittoria rarely share a bed and he is suspicious of the duke's intentions towards his wife. Flamineo advises him that the best cure for jealousy is to give his wife her freedom. In a comic passage full of **asides** and double meanings, he simultaneously persuades his brother-in-law to sleep alone and his sister to sleep with the duke. The duke and Vittoria lie down together and exchange 'jewels' (line 219). She relates her dream of the death of his wife and her husband. Flamineo comments, 'Excellent devil. / She hath taught him in a dream / To make away his duchess and her husband' (lines 254–6). But Brachiano says that he will interpret her dream 'Sweetly' (line 257) protect her and place her 'above law and above scandal' (line 261). They are interrupted by her mother, Cornelia. She accuses them of adultery and announces the arrival of the duchess in Rome. Their

> **CONTEXT**
>
> Dreams had long been analysed and interpreted as prophetic. In the Renaissance there were complex theories about their origins and meaning. Not all people were believers though. The writer Thomas Nashe thought a dream 'nothing else but a bubbling scum or froth of the fancy' (*The Terrors of the Night*, 1594), sig. C3v).

CONTEXT

One of the 'Beatitudes' (from Christ's most famous open-air sermon, which was delivered to a large crowd on a mountainside and recorded in the Gospel of St Matthew 5:7 and St Luke 6:17–49), says 'Blessed be ye poor: for yours is the kingdom of God.'

adultery, Cornelia foretells, will lead to their early deaths. She curses her daughter, who runs from the room. The duke is furious, accuses Cornelia of lack of charity and tells her that she will be responsible for what follows before storming out. Flamineo blames his mother for upsetting the duke and also for the disadvantages of his situation in life. Cornelia's response offers a conventionally moral Christian viewpoint that poverty is not a crime: 'What? Because we are poor, / Shall we be vicious?' (lines 312–13). But Flamineo demands to know, 'Pray what means have you / To keep me from the galleys or the gallows?' (lines 313–14). He complains that his father sold all their land, and spent the money before his death so that his children have to make their own way in the world as best they can. Cornelia exits in despair. Alone on stage Flamineo **soliloquises**, confiding that 'We are engaged in mischief and must on' (line 345) and that his way is to imitate 'The subtle foldings of a winter's snake' (line 350).

COMMENTARY

CONTEXT

Many plays in the period are centrally concerned with jealousy and masculine fears of a wife's infidelity and thus being made a 'cuckold' (line 69). *The White Devil* is full of jokes about cuckoldry and Flamineo elaborates on the idea at line 76 in his reference to 'horn-shavings' – cuckolds were popularly imagined to grow horns on their foreheads. Flamineo suggests that Camillo has shaved his off and stuffed his pillow with them.

This long, dramatic scene presents the main characters on stage for the first time and sets up the play's characteristic mixture of tone and style. In the previous scene Lodovico mentioned the Duke of Brachiano and his passion for Vittoria Corombona. We now meet them and witness the beginning of their love affair. Seeing her husband revealed as a fool and not an attractive or suitable mate, the audience may well sympathise with Vittoria. Despite their anomalous situation she and the duke see themselves as romantic lovers and use the discourse of **courtly love** in their relations. This is punctuated, however, by the **asides** of Zanche, Flamineo and Cornelia, all of whom witness the encounter. Their contrasting viewpoints offer a kaleidoscopic commentary which ranges from Zanche's romantic enthusiasm to Flamineo's cynicism and Cornelia's moral condemnation.

The love affair is the centre of the plot and the duke the most important character, but it is Flamineo, his secretary and Vittoria's brother, who dominates the scene. He is like a brilliant master of ceremonies orchestrating and manipulating people and events. His cynical commentary on characters and events in asides to the audience mark him out as an example of the **malcontent** in early modern drama. There is a bawdy, sexualised, misogynistic **subtext** present in all his talk, and however engaging as a character, to accept Flamineo's judgement is to collude in his cynicism and misogyny; women he says 'are like cursed dogs, civility keeps them tied all daytime, but they are let loose at midnight; then they do most good or most mischief' (lines 196–9).

At this point the audience will be confused. Everything the characters say seems ambiguous, capable of a very different construction from the one the hearer puts on it. This **ambiguity** works on many levels: it pervades the whole play with a sense of **irony**, creating at one level a bawdy subtext and at another it produces a systematic level of **dramatic irony** as characters' lightly spoken words ultimately reveal the deepest truths. For example in line 3, Brachiano complains that he is 'Quite lost', meaning either that he believes he has 'lost' the opportunity of being alone with Vittoria that night, or more generally that he has 'lost' himself because of his passion for her. In fact his passion signifies that he is mentally, morally and materially 'lost' and so the play proves.

When Flamineo is alone on stage he warns the audience what is going to happen: that the duchess's arrival will bring trouble. He relishes his villainy, 'We are engaged in mischief' (line 345) without specifying who 'We' are or the goal they seek to achieve. The imagery he uses of the 'winter snake' and 'winding' (lines 350, 352) path should alert the reader to the moral implications of leaving the 'straight and narrow path' appropriate for a Christian. Of course following the path of virtue does not make for exciting drama. As **Reading _The White Devil_** points out, drama is about conflict. Perhaps the most revealing **metaphor** for the play as a whole is the 'pair of spectacles fashioned with such perspective art' (lines 100–1) that to the wearer nothing is as it seems. This suggests the limited nature of human vision refracted through the prism of art and the difficulty of knowing what constitutes truth.

QUESTION

To what extent do you think the audience is likely to agree with Flamineo's argument and the decisions he has made?

CONTEXT

Perspective in art was first used in Renaissance painting. There has been considerable debate recently as to whether painters used special lenses and devices such as the _camera obscura_ to help them, largely sparked off by the research of the painter David Hockney and physicist Charles Falco. They argue that it was only by the use of such devices that artists such as Jan Van Eyck were able to achieve the high level of realism apparent in pictures such as _The Arnolfini Portrait_ (1434).

CONTEXT

The 'foot-cloth' (line 51) was a large richly-ornamented cloth laid over the back of a horse and hanging down to the ground on each side, considered a mark of dignity and state. Flamineo is implying that Camillo may be well-dressed but he is a fool underneath.

CONTEXT

Bowls had become so popular in Henry VIII's time that it was prohibited to all but the wealthy since working men were spending too much time playing. Henry was a keen player himself. James I banned football and golf but encouraged bowls. It was the source of many sexual and political **metaphors** in the period, for example at line 65 where 'bowl booty' means to cheat. The 'bias' (line 67) refers to the weight within the bowl causing it to swerve.

GLOSSARY

1	**Your best of rest** sleep well
8	**caroche** stately, luxurious coach
18	**superficies** outward form or aspect
21	**politic** cunning, clever, worldly-wise
22	**satiety** being glutted or full (of food)
23	**buttery-hatch** half-door over which provisions are served
25	**hot suit** urgent desire
28	**quicksilver** Mercury (quicksilver) a poisonous liquid metal which causes severe mental disorders was mixed with gold and used in gilding
	liver believed to be the seat of the passions
28–30	**barriers ... hairs** low fences ran down the centre of the places used for combat in tournaments, on which feathers from the contestants' helmets would often be struck off; Flamineo likens this to the way Camillo has lost his hair which he implies is from syphilis contracted through sexual encounters
31	**play ... downward** lose everything including the shirt off his back and then he would pawn everything below, especially his genitals, implying that Camillo has pawned his virility
32	**hazard** a game using dice
33	**Dutch doublet** tight-fitting jacket worn with padded breeches
35	**shroud** conceal, plays on sense of 'prepare for burial'
46	**consumption** wasting disease
57	**count** reckoning, puns on an expletive for female genitalia, sometimes spelled this way and similarly pronounced
59	**flaw** squall, breach, plays on bawdy sense of 'vagina'
66	**fain** gladly
68	**Aristotle** Greek philosopher, i.e. in spite of your learning
69	**ephemerides** astronomical almanacs
71	**Pew wew** exclamation expressing contempt or derision
74	**God boy you** contraction of 'God be with you'
81	**leon** leash for hounds
84	**in suspense** not yet executed (legal term)
86	**wrings** squeezes, i.e. because it is too tight for his asses' (large) ears

GLOSSARY

92	**capricious** puns on Latin *caper* meaning goat, an animal notorious for lechery
	mathematically precisely
	coxcomb fool (from the cap worn by professional fools in the shape of a 'cock's comb' with phallic innuendo)
94	**mutton** sheep, slang for 'prostitute'
95–6	**provocative electuaries** aphrodisiacs
96	**uttered** promoted
	Jubilee signified a year instituted by Pope Boniface in 1300 for obtaining indulgences for the remission of sins – 1600 was the most recent when the play was written
97	**physic** treat with medicine
100	**perspective** optical
111	**several** distinct
116	**snow of Ida** i.e. sheep's wool; Mount Ida near Troy was famous for sheep
	Corinth slang for 'brothel'; Greek town famed for its market of luxury goods and prostitutes
125	**carved** served, gave amorous signs
128	**capon** castrated cock
131	**black guard** lowest menial in a noble household
133	**tickle** chastise, ironically playing on sense of 'arouse'
135	**sage** wisdom
135–6	**crouching ... hams** bending the backs of the knees, i.e. begging
137	**itch** desire, plays on sense of irritation from venereal disease
	glass-house glass factory
160	**breese** gadflies
	tail penis
167	**tumultuary** irregular, undisciplined
168	*quae negata grata* what is denied is desired (Latin)
169	**adamant** fabulously hard, magnetic rock
173	**progress** official journey of monarch (or other dignitary) accompanied by nobles

continued

CONTEXT

A 'Jacob's staff' (line 94) was an instrument used for measuring heights and distances, called after the staff used by pilgrims visiting the shrine of Saint James, Santiago de Compostela in Spain.

CONTEXT

Enclosures (line 94) relates to the practice of enclosing common land for sheep farming, a cause of rural poverty and unrest, since those who did not own land then had nowhere to graze their animals.

CONTEXT

In his discussion of Vittoria's complexion in lines 118–19 which he compares to a 'blackbird's feather' (i.e. black) rather than its 'bill' (i.e. yellow) Flamineo is satirising conventional literary admiration of blond beauty and suggests that since she is brunette the duke will not be attracted to her.

CHECK THE BOOK

Alchemy was the chemistry of the middle ages and early modern period. The philosopher's stone (line 152) was the mythical object of the alchemist's search to turn base metals into gold and prolong life indefinitely. At II.2.82 it is referred to as 'coz'ning' (cheating) alchemy since so many practitioners were rogues and devised various ingenious scams to defraud the public. Ben Jonson's play *The Alchemist* (1610) is a brilliant **satire** on the alchemist as con artist.

GLOSSARY

184	**gull** cheat
189	**scurvily** meanly, rudely
216	**pander** pimp
232	**yew-tree** evergreen tree often planted in churchyards, symbols of sadness
235	**cross-sticks** exact meaning unclear, 'cross' probably suggests an ill omen
245	**fury** avenging spirit in Greek mythology
273	**Thessaly** region of northern Greece
285	**dials** sundials, clocks
290	**blood** family lineage, bloodshed, desire
311–12	**bear … stirrup** meaning not have to walk humbly by my lord's horse
318	**Padua** city containing the oldest university in Italy
321–2	**conspiring … graduate** exact meaning unclear but suggests he was engaged in some illicit activity in order to graduate
325	**suit** of clothes, legal work, preferment
340	**Lycurgus** distinguished Athenian orator and statesman (c.390–c.325 BC)
350	**winter's snake** reptiles move slowly in winter; plays on biblical sense of 'snake' as immoral

ACT II

SCENE 1

- Isabella, Brachiano's wife, has arrived in Rome with their son, Giovanni, hoping to be reconciled with her husband.
- Cardinal Monticelso (Camillo's uncle) and Francisco (Isabella's brother) accuse Brachiano of making Vittoria his whore.
- Brachiano rejects Isabella and divorces her in private.
- Isabella publicly play-acts divorcing her husband.
- Flamineo has found a doctor to poison Isabella and says that he will personally take care of Camillo.
- Camillo and Marcello receive their commission to capture Lodovico.

Learning of her husband's affair with Vittoria, Isabella has arrived in Rome with her son, Giovanni, to visit her brother, Francisco, the duke of Florence, and try to achieve a reconciliation with Brachiano. Vittoria and Flamineo's brother, Marcello, a soldier in Francisco's army, announces Brachiano's arrival and takes Giovanni to find him a suit of armour. Francisco tells Isabella to hide. She is convinced she can win back her husband's affections and tells Francisco that, in the same way men test the efficacy of unicorn's horn as a protection against the poison of spiders by making a circle around them, 'so these arms / Shall charm his poison' (lines 16–17).

As soon as Brachiano enters, Francisco orders the others to 'Void the chamber' (line 19). He and Cardinal Monticelso then try to persuade Brachiano to give up Vittoria, appealing to his pride – he's drunk but will soon be sober and 'when you wake from this lascivious dream, / Repentance then will follow' (lines 35–6). He is an 'eagle' (i.e. king of birds) but Vittoria is socially inferior. Francisco angrily accuses him 'She is your strumpet' (line 58). Brachiano is defiant, saying he would rather go to war than give Vittoria up. Francisco regrets giving Brachiano his sister's hand in marriage. Monticelso tries to make peace. Francisco complains that Brachiano is neglecting his duties and engaged with whores. When

CHECK THE NET

Francisco complains that although her husband 'is lord of a poor fortune' Vittoria 'wears cloth of tissue' (lines 54–5), that is she's dressing above her station in life, a common complaint at the time. Tudor sumptuary laws laid down what members of each social class were allowed to wear. Much of the disquiet around the theatres related to the fact that common actors dressed as kings and nobles, not to mention women, thus flouting established dress codes. Go to **www.elizabethan. org** for more information on sumptuary laws and Elizabethan cultural practices.

CONTEXT

Francisco likens his brother-in-law's fate to that of melancholic 'stags' (line 94); male deer were supposed to leave the herd to die alone after mating so Francisco is playing on the idea of the cuckold's horns.

CONTEXT

Marriage between aristocrats was basically a political arrangement and women were often used to cement alliances. Divorce from bed and board (*a mensa et thoro*) could be granted on the grounds of adultery. It was in effect legalised separation, meaning that the marriage bond was technically unbroken and the parties were not free to remarry.

Giovanni enters in his armour Monticelso sees him as an instrument of peace to unite the brothers-in-law, 'here comes a champion / Shall end the difference between you both … this is a casket / For both your crowns, and should be held like [as] dear' (lines 95–9). Francisco calls for Camillo in order to discuss with him the capture of Lodovico, who has become a pirate. However, Isabella enters and Francisco leaves her alone with Brachiano, hoping they will be reconciled.

Isabella tries to win her husband back but he is angry and refuses to kiss her, cruelly rejecting her attempts to embrace her exclaiming 'O your breath!' (line 163). She reminds him of their past love but he accuses her of stirring up her brother to make war, or of visiting a lover in Rome. Furthermore, he blames Francisco for their marriage, cursing him as well as 'the priest / That sang the wedding mass, and even my issue' (lines 190–1), that is their son, Giovanni. Isabella is distressed, 'O too too far you have cursed' (line 192). Brachiano then divorces her in a **parody** of the marriage ceremony (lines 192–8).

Isabella begs Brachiano to change his mind but he is unmoved and tells her to complain to her brother. She says that to make peace between them she will pretend that she is the one who has brought about the separation. When her brother and the cardinal return she playacts a scene in which she pretends that it is she who has rejected him. She speaks angrily, threatening to 'dig the strumpet's eyes out' (line 245). The men are fooled and blame Isabella's fury for the failure of her marriage, 'Now by my birth you are a foolish, mad, / And jealous woman' (lines 263–4).

Marcello tells Francisco that Camillo has arrived about the commission to capture Lodovico, and while Francisco, Marcello and Camillo talk, Flamineo and Brachiano discuss Isabella's poisoning with Doctor Julio; Flamineo says he will take care of his brother-in-law himself. Monticelso gives Camillo a paper with an emblem of a stag which has lost its horns. He tells him he is thought to be a cuckold and that Vittoria is unfaithful to him. Camillo objects that his going away will give Vittoria more opportunity but Monticelso says he will watch over her. When Camillo has gone Monticelso and Francisco reveal their plan to destroy Brachiano because of the scandal of his affair with Vittoria. Francisco uses the **simile** of the parasitic 'mistletoe' (line 396) to describe the relationship between Vittoria and Brachiano.

COMMENTARY

All the comings and goings in this busy scene suggest that it has been contrived in order to force a showdown between Brachiano and his opponents – his wife, her brother and the cardinal. The dialogue between Francisco and Monticelso, reprimanding Brachiano, recalls the opening scene in which Gasparo and Antonelli chided Lodovico. The clearing of the chamber recalls Brachiano's entrance in the previous scene. There we saw Brachiano infatuated by Vittoria's beauty, now we see him rejecting his wife, Isabella. The two women offer a complete contrast with each other. The scene highlights one of the play's major themes, the conflict between marriage, a relationship based on political and financial interests, and passion and sexual desire.

Isabella, who is represented as pious and virtuous, is nevertheless able to act a scene of public fury convincingly. Her **aside** makes it clear that she has done this for her husband's sake despite the heart-break it causes her: 'Unkindness do thy office, poor heart break, / Those are the killing griefs which dare not speak' (lines 276–7). However, we are bound to ask to what extent her outburst reveals her true feelings. Her brother's response demonstrates how quick men are to blame women for everything.

The scene also foreshadows future events. The two powerful dukes make plans in which they unscrupulously employ others to achieve their aims. Francisco hopes to ruin Brachiano through the developing scandal of his affair with Vittoria, and Monticelso is already talking of revenge, while Brachiano and Flamineo discuss the murders of Isabella and Camillo. It is full of the animal imagery characteristic of Webster and intended as a sign of characters falling below the level of the human. The first appearance of young Giovanni is important too. In contrast to the older men he is lively and precocious and they treat him with affection. His father calls him 'Forward lapwing' (line 25), his uncle 'Pretty cousin' (line 27) and Monticelso 'Witty prince' (line 37).

> **CONTEXT**
>
> Webster is well-known for his use of animal **imagery**, which is used **ironically** and implies that characters have become less than human. Francisco talks about Camillo's house as a 'dove-house' (line 3) – the dove is a traditional symbol of peace and innocence, which he suggests is haunted by predatory 'pole-cats' (line 5), known for their foul smell (also meaning 'prostitutes').

CHECK THE BOOK

Falconry or hawking was a popular aristocratic pastime. It provided many literary sporting **metaphors** for example at III.2.38 when Vittoria complains that the lawyer's words, 'Come up like stones we use give hawks for physic' meaning they are vomited up in the same way as stones are that are given to hawks as medicine.

CHECK THE BOOK

In this scene, the reference to '**tale of a tub**' (line 92) plays on the 'sweating tub' used to cure venereal disease. *A Tale of a Tub*, meaning a trivial tale, is the title of a play by Ben Jonson (performed in 1633) in which he satirises Inigo Jones who designed many of his court masques. It is also the title of satirist Jonathan Swift's controversial political religious satire, *A Tale of a Tub* (1704).

GLOSSARY

46	**fetch a course about** retreat, i.e. from what has been said in a cowardly way
51	**dunghill birds** inferior birds who scavenge offal
52–3	**shift ... tennis** meaning that the duke uses her house to change his clothes, suggesting intimacy
53	**Happily** perhaps/with pleasure
56	**shrift** confession to a priest
59	**hemlock** poison
61	**borrowed Switzers** hired Swiss mercenaries
68	**Thy ghostly ... absolution** the priest with all his authority to forgive sins
73	**but crackers** merely fireworks/boasts
76	**perfumes for plasters** sweet smells for bandages used to treat venereal disease
78	**new-ploughed** as in furrowed with anger
82	**triumph** ancient Roman festivity in which lions were baited to make them fight
88	**prowling passenger** passing hawk, especially peregrine falcon
89	**wild ducks** prey, prostitutes
90	**moulting time** when birds shed their plumage or people their hair, implying as a symptom of venereal disease
93	**express ... reason** explain using common sense
94	**season** appropriate time
109	**pike** spear with a metal tip, penis
111	**Homer's frogs ... bullrush** from *The Battle of Frogs and Mice* a mock epic in which the frogs use bulrushes as pikes
119	**Dansk** Danish
125	**lapwing** bird, regarded as precocious, who could fly from the moment it was hatched
161	**Italian** Italian emotion, i.e. jealousy
166	**cassia** expensive perfume
172	**bandy factions** i.e. form my enemies into groups
177	**supply our discontinuance** do what I no longer do, i.e. sexually
181–3	**rest upon record** be public knowledge

GLOSSARY

183	**Like ... Polack** meaning as being of no importance; Poles were said to be careless of life and to shave their heads completely except for a long forelock
193	**latest** last, final
205	**winding sheet** shroud, sheet in which a corpse is buried; Isabella is ironically correct although she means that she will die from grief
219	**weal** happiness, prosperity
262	***manet ... repostum*** it shall be treasured up in the depths of my mind (Virgil, *Aeneid*, I.26)
272	**stomach** pride, obstinacy, anger
275	**turn in post** quickly return
281	**signet** ring for sealing the commission
284	**stibium** metallic compound used as poison
284–5	**cantharides** dried beetle or Spanish fly, considered an aphrodisiac
290	**Candy** i.e. death; it was said that the inhabitants of Candia (now Crete) lived on serpents
	property i.e. stage prop for Flamineo and Brachiano's 'play'
292	**quack-salving knave** charlatan who concocts bogus medicines
296	**cozened** cheated
297	**colourable execution** plausible judgement
299	**ventages ... lamprey** lampreys are eel-like fish with apertures (ventages) on the sides of the head
301	**Ireland ... poison** refers to the story that St Patrick supposedly banished all the snakes from Ireland
304	**St Anthony's fire** inflammatory skin disease; possibly slang for 'breaking wind'
307	**chirurgeon** surgeon
309–10	**gargarism** gargle
310	**lights** lungs
311	**scruples** small quantities
317	**engine** device, contrivance
323	**emblem** drawing illustrating a moral fable or allegory
337, 342	**Mercury ... Jupiter/Jove** respectively the messenger and chief of the Roman gods
345	**bans** banns, announcing marriage

continued

CHECK THE POEM

Virgil (70–19BCE) was the most popular and influential classical poet in the middle ages and the Renaissance. Born Publius Vergilius Maro he wrote a series of bucolic poems (or *Eclogues*) set in a mythical Arcadia, the *Georgics* (related to farming and the land) and his twelve book epic on the foundation of Rome by Aeneas, the *Aeneid*, in which Virgil attempted to create a Latin work to match the Greek epics of Homer, the *Iliad* and *Odyssey*.

CHECK THE BOOK

In Shakespeare's *Measure for Measure* another Isabella defends her virtue proclaiming 'Th'impression of keen whips I'd wear as rubies / And strip myself to death, as to a bed / That longing have been sick for, ere I'd yield / My body up to shame' (II.4.105–8).

CONTEXT

Francisco's lengthy recital (lines 334–55) is one of a number of mythological tales from *The Fables of Aesop* (1596). It tells the bizarre story of the response of those who have to work in the heat such as 'smiths' and 'cooks' to the news of the marriage of the sun god Phoebus and their anxiety that if he were allowed to reproduce the heat would be intolerable. As so often in Webster's application of the tales, the speaker twists the meaning in an unexpected way which leaves the audience confused and unconvinced. Francisco uses it to suggest that Vittoria is Phoebus and people would be sorry if she had children.

GLOSSARY

347 **gelded** castrated

358 **cornucopia** horn of plenty, usually a symbol of fertility, used ironically of Camillo's cuckold's horns

364 **ranger** game-keeper, rake or libertine

384 **sister Duchess** a courtesy title; Monticelso is Camillo's uncle, unless Webster is confused with the real life Cardinal de Medici who was Isabella's brother

396 **sere** dry, withered

SCENE 2

- A Conjuror shows Brachiano the deaths of his wife and Camillo in dumb shows.

It is midnight and Brachiano reminds a Conjuror that he has promised to show him the deaths of Camillo and his duchess. The Conjuror describes the tricks that those practising his art are able to perform before telling Brachiano to put on a 'charmed' (line 21) night-cap which will enable him to see the duchess's death. In the first **dumb show**, Doctor Julio and his assistant Christophero treat with poison a portrait of Brachiano which Isabella kisses on her way to bed. She dies and Giovanni and Lodovico grieve for her. Brachiano's chilling response is, 'Excellent, then she's dead' (line 24). He notices and questions the presence of Count Lodovico. In the second dumb show Flamineo, Marcello, Camillo and others are drinking and dancing. A vaulting horse is brought in and while Marcello is out of the room Flamineo pitches Camillo, who is preparing to vault, on to his neck, breaking it. They call for help; Marcello arrives, sends for Francisco and the cardinal who arrest Flamineo and Marcello and go to arrest Vittoria. Brachiano is delighted with what he has seen, ''Twas quaintly done' (line 38) and pays the Conjuror handsomely.

COMMENTARY

This scene is an economical way of showing us events and their outcome. The two dumb shows are deliberately distanced and stylised

– attention is drawn to their theatricality by the presence of Brachiano and the Conjuror watching the scenes. The audience watch them watching. The only dialogue is between Brachiano and the Conjuror. The time and situation are full of horror and the silent events macabre. The detailed stage directions, including the putting on of spectacles and the laughter of Julio and his accomplice, add to the horror.

GLOSSARY

7	**sophistic** cunning
8	**nigromancer** i.e. 'necromancer' meaning one who predicts the future by communicating with the dead; this form suggests one who practises black magic, from *niger* black (Latin)
9	**juggle** play tricks, cheat
12	**windmills** fanciful schemes or projects
13	**quib** small firework
16	**figure-flingers** (contemptuous term) casters of horoscopes
19–20	**They'd … Latin** meaning that by speaking inflated Latin they'd make people believe they had conjured up the devil
	fast and loose slippery, inconstant; originally a cheating game
25	**fumed** exposed to ammonia vapour
28	**dead shadow** lifeless image
37	(stage direction 3) *whispered … room* got out of the room on some whispered pretext
38	**quaintly** neatly, skilfully
39	**taste** understand/enjoy
40	**boon voyage** prosperous journey, as in '*bon voyage*'
46	**engine** here ingenuity, genius
51	**postern** door, gate

CONTEXT

It was during this period that science and magic began to be distinguished from each other as they are today. Before that natural scientists also practised astrology and alchemy. Dr John Dee was the most famous mathematician, physician and magician of the day and became Elizabeth I's advisor on scientific and astrological matters.

CONTEXT

The reference at lines 13–15 to keeping a 'curtal to show juggling tricks' is one of numerous contemporary English references which relate the play to Webster's London. In the 1590s a travelling showman, Mr Banks, exhibited his performing horse which he had trained to dance, count money and play dead. From 1595 he was using a bay gelding with a docked tail or 'curtal' called Morocco.

CONTEXT

A 'lieger'
Ambassador, such as
those who witness
the trial of Vittoria,
was a high-ranking
minister
permanently
resident at a foreign
court who
represents his
sovereign or
country, and has a
right to a personal
interview with the
sovereign or chief
magistrate of the
country in which he
resides.

ACT III

SCENE 1

- Vittoria is to be put on trial for the murder of her husband.
- Francisco congratulates Monticelso on arranging for the foreign Ambassadors to attend.
- Marcello blames Flamineo for Vittoria's situation and urges him to become honest.
- The Ambassadors arrive.

Francisco congratulates Monticelso on persuading the foreign Ambassadors to attend Vittoria's trial which will give it authority. Monticelso thinks it essential since they have only circumstantial evidence for her involvement in her husband's death and hope to ruin her reputation abroad. He questions whether Brachiano will attend but Francisco thinks he will not dare. Flamineo and Marcello enter under guard with a lawyer. Flamineo claims that his 'feigned garb of mirth' (line 29) is to avoid suspicion.

**www. CHECK
THE NET**
One of the most
famous paintings of
the Renaissance is
Hans Holbein's *The
Ambassadors* (1533).
You can find it
reproduced at
**www.national
gallery.org.uk** –
put 'Holbein
Ambassadors' into
the search box. Note
especially the strange
disc-shaped object in
the foreground which
is an anamorphic
(meaning using an
oblique perspective)
representation of a
skull, a *memento
mori* to remind the
spectator of the
presence of death.

Marcello wishes that he had killed Vittoria when she first saw Brachiano and accuses his brother of being 'his engine, and his stalking-horse / To undo my sister' (lines 33–4). Flamineo defends himself, 'I made a kind of path / To her and mine own preferment' (lines 34–5), in other words, he acted in the best interests of himself and his sister, pointing out that Marcello serves Francisco with his 'prodigal blood' but his only reward is 'a poor handful' (lines 40–41). Marcello rejects Flamineo's ideas and begs him to reform, claiming that 'an honest heart' (line 56) is the best inheritance. The three Ambassadors arrive and Flamineo makes **satirical** comments about their character and appearance.

COMMENTARY

This short scene forms the prelude to the Arraignment. It enables the audience to discover the contrasting thoughts of different characters. Francisco and Monticelso (unaware as yet of Isabella's death) hope to put an end to Vittoria's affair with Brachiano by ruining her reputation. Flamineo and Marcello disagree profoundly about their situation and reveal the stark choice before Vittoria. The innocent Marcello adheres to traditional notions of honour in which he would have had the right to kill his sister for dishonouring the family name. The guilty Flamineo defends his actions and points out that Marcello's virtuous path has proved unprofitable.

CHECK THE BOOK

Robert Greene was one of the so-called 'University Wits' young men who had been to university – there were only two at this time, Oxford and Cambridge – and supported themselves by writing. He is said to have been the first professional English writer. His most successful publications were his 'coney-catching' pamphlets such as *A Disputation Between a Hee Conny-Catcher and a Shee Conny-Catcher* (1592) which related various scams and sharp practices from the perspective of a repentant criminal.

GLOSSARY		
11	**in by the week**	caught, trapped
12	**sit upon**	sit in judgement upon; with obscene sense of 'mount for sex'
14–15	**tickler**	punisher, chastiser/provoker
16	**tilting**	jousting/copulating
17	**private**	secretive, intimate
19	**public**	indiscreet/licentious; a 'public woman' is a prostitute
21	**ferret**	hunt with ferrets, especially rabbits, i.e. discover, bring to light
22	**catch conies**	slang term meaning 'cheat fools'; 'conies' are literally 'rabbits' but also used of women as a term of endearment or with an obscene meaning
28	**lighted**	arrived, alighted from their horses or carriages
38	**serviceable**	ready to serve; witches were believed to breastfeed their familiars or spirits (sent from the devil) with milk or blood
40	**wealth of captains**	soldiers were proverbially poor
41	**palm**	'bearing the palm' is a term for gaining victory
44	**chamois**	soft leather jerkins, worn under armour

continued

CONTEXT

A 'stalking-horse' (line 33) was originally a horse trained to allow a fowler to conceal himself behind it or under its coverings in order to get within easy range of game without alarming it; **metaphorically** it could mean one whose action or participation is designed to prevent its real design from being suspected.

GLOSSARY

48-50 **mistletoe ... mandrake** mistletoe was believed to have medical properties when growing on an oak tree, whereas the mandrake plant, whose forked root was said to feed on blood, was often found near gallows and was regarded as poisonous; the sense is that good and bad are to be found close together

51–2 **Alas ... strikes** great men may appear to punish a mild offence lightly but in fact they will destroy the offender completely

57 **respect** scheme

73 **carries ... ruff** mocks the Spanish fashion for large ruffs

74 **cypress** crepe, fine material

SCENE 2 – The Arraignment of Vittoria

- Brachiano arrives to witness Vittoria's arraignment (accusation before a tribunal).
- Vittoria objects to the lawyer's Latin and legal jargon; Monticelso accuses her in plain English.
- Brachiano intervenes, argues with Monticelso and leaves.
- Francisco admits there is no evidence of Vittoria's involvement in the murder but Monticelso accuses her of immorality and Vittoria defends herself.
- Flamineo and Marcello are discharged but Vittoria is punished by being sent with Zanche to a house of convertites.
- Brachiano returns to offer Francisco his friendship.
- Flamineo decides to pretend to be mad; Giovanni and Lodovico arrive and announce Isabella's death.

CONTEXT

At this time, when the Church was an important part of the organisation and regulation of society, religious and moral offences were tried in Ecclesiastical Courts – often known as 'bawdy courts'. They typically dealt with cases of fornication, adultery, defamation of character, slander, rowdy behaviour, Sunday working or drinking, heresy, witchcraft, usury, incest and neglect of religious observance.

Monticelso objects that there is no place for Brachiano who then lays his cloak on the ground, recalling his first encounter with Vittoria in Act I Scene 2, when a carpet is spread on the floor. The lawyer charges Vittoria in Latin but she objects defiantly, claiming, 'I will not have my application clouded / In a strange tongue: all this assembly / Shall hear what you charge me with' (lines 18–20). The lawyer then speaks in legal jargon full of latinate terms to which Vittoria also objects. Monticelso takes up the case and insults Vittoria (lines 51–3).

Vittoria responds by arguing that churchmen should not be lawyers (lines 59–61), and uses her wit **ironically** against Monticelso as he accuses her bitterly, 'O poor charity! / Thou art seldom found in scarlet' (lines 71–2). In his fury Monticelso calls her 'whore' (line 78) and angrily expounds the term to her but Vittoria simply retorts 'This character scapes me' (line 102). He continues by asserting that after 'whore' 'next the devil, Adult'ry' then 'Murder' (line 108–9) naturally follow. She kneels humbly before the Ambassadors, who form an impartial audience to the trial, apologising that she is forced to defend herself like a man but proudly proclaims that if found guilty she is not afraid to die and will not beg for her life (lines 138–9). As the English Ambassador remarks, 'She hath a brave spirit' (line 140). Vittoria rejects the cardinal's accusations, calling them 'feigned shadows of my evils' (line 146). His jibes are wasted on her and will only rebound on him (lines 147–51).

Monticelso then asks directly who was in her house the night her husband died and Brachiano says he was there to comfort Vittoria for fear that Monticelso would cheat her of the money her husband owed him: it was from charity but Monticelso says it was from 'lust'. Brachiano angrily threatens to destroy Monticelso before storming out. Monticelso tells Vittoria 'Your champion's gone' to which she responds 'The wolf may prey the better' (line 180). Francisco points out to Monticelso that although Camillo's death was suspicious there is no evidence against Vittoria.

Monticelso then produces a letter from Brachiano, arranging to meet Vittoria, but she argues that does not make her guilty. She cannot be held responsible for the duke loving her, 'So may you blame some fair and crystal river / For that some melancholic distracted man / Hath drowned himself in't' (lines 204–6). All she can actually be charged with is enjoying herself (lines 207–10).

CHECK THE BOOK

The Lawyer's use of the word 'connive' (line 27) is an example of a comic device known as a 'malapropism' – accidentally substituting a word which looks and sounds similar to the correct one. The term comes from Richard Brinsley Sheridan's play *The Rivals* (1775) in which a character called Mrs Malaprop does this all the time, to great comic effect, confusing 'alligators' and 'allegories' for example. It was a technique which other writers had already employed, notably Shakespeare with the character of Dogberry in *Much Ado About Nothing* or Mistress Quickly in the *Henry IV* plays and *The Merry Wives of Windsor.*

SCENE 2 – THE ARRAIGNMENT OF VITTORIA continued

CONTEXT

English law courts at this period used the Law French instituted by William the Conqueror after the Norman Conquest. It was based on Anglo–Norman and its use became increasingly artificial as English became the native tongue of the aristocracy. Certain Law French terms have entered common parlance however such as 'mortgage' literally 'dead pledge', or 'torts' that is 'wrongs'.

CONTEXT

This was the period which saw the beginnings of the science of anatomy. The reference at lines 97–9, 'dead ... surgeons' is to the practice in which the Company of Barber Surgeons were allowed four bodies per year of convicted felons for anatomical dissection; they may have 'begged' extra corpses.

Monticelso says that the duke gave her money but she says it was to save her husband from prison and challenges him if he is to be her accuser to cease pretending to be her judge. Monticelso recites the story of her courtship and marriage to Camillo who he says spent 'in six months / Twelve thousand ducats, and to my acquaintance / Received in dowry with you not one julio' (lines 239–41). She is, he continues, 'a most notorious strumpet' (line 244). He dismisses the charges against Flamineo and Marcello, and sentences Vittoria to be confined with Zanche, her 'bawd' (261) to a house of convertites. Vittoria angrily denounces the judgement calling it 'A rape, a rape!' (line 273), claiming that Monticelso has 'ravished Justice' (line 274). But then she recollects herself and in a speech of superb pride announces that her will and her presence have the power to overcome his doom (lines 289–94).

Brachiano re-enters and makes peace with Francisco before leaving again. This Flamineo interprets as a precaution before he hears of Isabella's death. Flamineo says that he himself will feign madness. Giovanni and Count Lodovico enter and announce Isabella's death. Giovanni asks Francisco about the meaning of death, 'What do the dead do, uncle?' (line 223) and recounts his own and his mother's suffering and how he loved her. Francisco is overcome with grief 'O all of my poor sister that remains! / Take him away for god's sake—' (lines 338–9). In response to Monticelso's question, he vows to 'keep her blessed memory / Longer than thousand epitaphs' (lines 341–2).

COMMENTARY

This is the central scene of the play, and its importance is signified unusually by a title 'The Arraignment of Vittoria' and Vittoria dominates it as she is confronted by and defends herself against the combined forces of Cardinal Monticelso and Francisco, duke of Florence. Her performance in the scene is remarkable for its rhetorical sophistication, confidence and assurance:

> Sum up my faults I pray, and you shall find
> That beauty and gay clothes, a merry heart,
> And a good stomach to feast, are all,

All the poor crimes that you can charge me with …
(lines 207–10)

Despite winning the verbal battles with Monticelso, Vittoria is condemned to be detained in the house of convertites, the house for 'penitent whores' (line 267). As the only one tried and condemned for the death of her husband, the audience is bound to feel that she has been unjustly treated, especially in contrast to Brachiano and Flamineo who we know to be guilty. It suggests that as a woman she was the easier target and that Brachiano, and Flamineo who is under his protection, are too powerful to be accused directly. Audience response is complicated by the fact that they know that Vittoria is guilty of adultery with Brachiano and further that her dream suggested the murders to him in the first place.

CONTEXT

Rhetoric, which originally meant the art of public speaking, was the backbone of humanist education in the grammar schools. From its beginnings in classical Greece rhetoric was taken to Rome where it dominated the teaching syllabus. As an art of persuasion it offered particularly useful training for lawyers and playwrights since they learned to see a case or situation from all points of view.

GLOSSARY

10–11	*Domine … corruptissimam* 'Lord Judge, turn your eyes upon this plague, the most corrupted of women'
23	have at you the lawyer threatens Vittoria as though he was going to shoot her
24	give aim guide (as in archery)
28	diversivolent desiring strife
29	concatenation linking together
30	extirp exterminate, root out
31	projections projects
36	pothecary's bills long-winded prescriptions
40	tropes nor figures in rhetoric, figurative use of words or phrases
46	fustian coarse cloth; inflated, bombastic language
47	buckram stiffened coarse cloth traditionally used for lawyers' bags; a stiff, starched manner
49	graduatically as a graduate should – a word made-up for the occasion
51–3	plainer … cheek the cardinal is implying that Vittoria's colour is not natural, that she is a 'painted' woman – a misogynistic stereotype

continued

CHECK THE BOOK

In classical mythology Perseus was the hero who slew the Gorgon, Medusa, a monster whose look turned all to stone. He used a mirror and cut off Medusa's head then destroyed his enemies by turning the head towards them. The passage in which Vittoria apologises for having to defend herself like a man ('personate … point' line 36, i.e. imitate masculine courage in every respect) may refer to Jonson's *Masque of Queens* (1609) in which Perseus represented 'heroic and masculine virtue'.

GLOSSARY

64–7   **apples … ashes** In the biblical story (Deuteronomy 32:32) the grapes of these cities destroyed by God for their evil ways were said to taste bitter; the turning of 'apples' to ashes is an addition by later writers

72   **scarlet** colour worn by cardinals and lawyers; implies they are rarely charitable

80   **character** description of a character-type; Webster contributed a number to Overbury's *New Characters* (1615)

87   **Worse … paid** very high taxes costing more than the goods themselves

90–2   **brittle … syllable** flimsy legal cases in which the whole estate might be forfeited if a word was accidentally left out

102   **scapes** does not describe; is unintelligible to

112   **Now … nothing** i.e. now that he's dead he has no debts

116   **rushes** a type of plant, commonly strewn on the floor in private homes and on stage, they should have created a soft landing for Camillo

122   **mourning habit** clothes appropriate to a widow mourning her husband's death, implying that Vittoria is finely dressed

124   **bespoke** ordered to be made

128   **Christian** ecclesiastical, civilised (used ironically)

129   **uncivil Tartar** uncivilised courts of the Tartars of central Asia reputedly barbarous and cruel

135   **force** necessity

143   **strict combined heads** closely allied forces, literally hammer-heads

148   **palsy** weakness, trembling (from fear)

164   **Sirrah** term of address used to an inferior

168   **thy** Brachiano has changed to the familiar personal pronoun often used to inferiors as a deliberate insult

        coat i.e. profession

177   **Valance** drape for the canopy around a bed

        demi-foot-cloth half-length covering for a horse

178   **moil** mule (traditional mount for a cardinal) playing on 'moil' drudgery

179   *Nemo me impune lacessit* 'No one wounds me with impunity' (Latin)

200   *Casta est quam nemo rogavit* 'She is chaste whom no man has solicited' (Ovid, *Amores* I, viii, 43); Vittoria ironically uses Latin

GLOSSARY

202	**dog-days** time when malignant influences prevail; literally, the hottest time of year when Sirius, the dog star, is high in the sky
215	**crusadoes** Portuguese coins bearing a cross
216–7	**devil … picture** a reference to the play's title: 'Satan himself is changed into an angel of light' (2 Corinthians, xi.14)
223	**use** interest
234	**choke-pear** rough, unpalatable variety of pear; severe reproof
	grafting in horticulture a form of reproduction by inserting a shoot of one plant into another stock – with bawdy innuendo
240	**ducats** gold coins of the Venetian Republic
241	**julio** small silver coin
248	**ordinary** common, customary, public house
249	**ballated** turned into a ballad, hence made common knowledge
254	**sureties** bail
272	**patent** special licence
276	**maws** throats, gullets
281	**horse-leech** i.e. blood-sucker
333	**fold of lead** lead-covering to preserve the body
335	**gave me suck** i.e. suckled me herself, very rare among the aristocracy

CHECK THE POEM

In *Paradise Lost*, Book One (1667), John Milton describes how the Devil corrupted Eve in the Garden of Eden: 'The infernal Serpent; he it was whose guile / Stirr'd up with envy and revenge deceived / The Mother of mankind.' In the play, however, Monticelso invokes Eve as the cause of man's fall from grace, and suggests that 'Were there a second paradise to lose / This devil would betray it' (70–1), 'This devil' being Vittoria.

SCENE 3

CHECK THE BOOK

The idea of worshipping gold as a god (line 21) is biblical in origin, for example **personified** as Mammon in the Sermon on the Mount in the New Testament (Matthew 5:7). Ben Jonson's satire *Volpone* (1607) opens with his protagonist proclaiming: 'Good morning to the day; and, next, my gold! / Open the shrine, that I may see my saint' (I.1.1–2).

CONTEXT

Blood-letting or phlebotomy was common in medical practice up to the nineteenth century. It involved opening a vein and allowing blood to drain off which was caught in a 'saucer' (line 89), the receptacle used for receiving blood.

SCENE 3

- Flamineo, pretending to be mad, expresses bitterness about the court's judgement.

- Flamineo and Lodovico form a pact.

- Lodovico learns that he has been pardoned by the old Pope on his deathbed and is delighted.

- Flamineo and Lodovico quarrel and fight.

The action of all three scenes in Act III is continuous. Flamineo, putting on the act of madness he promised in the previous scene, is bitter at the injustice of the judgement and his lack of reward: 'Is this the end of service?' (line 3).

The Ambassadors attempt to reconcile him to the verdict but he blames firstly politicians, then money and lastly the cardinal's corruption of the law (lines 15–23), before walking out.

Flamineo re-enters and reveals his suspicion of Lodovico, believing him to be linked to Isabella and Giovanni. Flamineo greets Lodovico – in an **aside** Marcello warns the audience to 'Mark this strange encounter' (line 65). Flamineo and Lodovico share their sense of grievance against the world. They make a pact 'Shalt thou and I join housekeeping?' and discuss how they will be 'unsociably sociable' (lines 75–6) together. Antonelli and Gasparo arrive with news that at Francisco's request the Pope on his deathbed has pardoned Lodovico. Flamineo is even more resentful and incensed at the news and Lodovico's pleasure: 'You shall not seem a happier man than I' (line 103). He and Lodovico taunt each other and Flamineo strikes him. They fight and are parted by Marcello, Antonelli and Gasparo.

COMMENTARY

Flamineo has said in the previous scene that 'Because now I cannot counterfeit a whining passion for the death of my lady, I will feign a mad humour for the disgrace of my sister, and that will keep off idle questions' (lines 304–7). Feigning madness was a common feature of **revenge tragedy** (the most well-known example being *Hamlet*) and engaging in wild talk with a **satirical** undertone. Flamineo becomes 'distracted' here, another term for madness, in order to deceive his enemies. His temporary alliance with Lodovico seems appropriate since they are parallel characters in many ways. The scene seems to exemplify the workings of the wheel of Fortune (it begins with Flamineo's complaint, 'We endure the spokes like anvils or hard steel', line 1) as Vittoria's and Flamineo's fortunes are at the bottom now while Lodovico's are suddenly restored. However in both cases, powerful human agency is seen to be responsible for this state of affairs. Lodovico's casual dismissal of Flamineo as one of 'These rogues that are most weary of their lives' (128) offers a piercingly accurate analysis of his condition – shared by Lodovico himself.

GLOSSARY	
5	**ostler** groom, stable-boy
	linings underclothing
6–7	**forty … Poland** the country was noted for its poverty
9	**built … piles** i.e. founded on the cure of syphilis as well as haemorrhoids, with a pun on 'piles', the timber foundations necessary in Venice
12–14	**They … them** a translation of lines from Seneca *Epistles* 109, 7, suggesting that words of comfort will not help one as deeply wounded as Flamineo
25	**gudgeons** small fish used for bait; credulous gullible persons
27	**victual … line** food at the equator, i.e. in the heat
30	**salary** reward
39–40	**first … religion** a reference to Cain's murder of his brother Abel, in a quarrel about how best to worship God, foreshadowing Flamineo's murder of Marcello
	Jew synonymous with money-lender
46–7	**priests … benefices** the passage satirises widespread abuse in which a single clergyman held several offices
	continued

CONTEXT

The reference to 'those weights they press men to death with' (lines 28–9) relates to the English practice known as 'torture of the press' (*peine forte et dure*) in which prisoners who refused to plead at trial were starved and crushed slowly under heavy iron weights. Their property, however, could not be confiscated since they could not be convicted.

CONTEXT

Torture was used routinely at this period to extract confessions, for example at line 35 Flamineo talks about being 'racked', that is tortured on the rack. This was a frame with a roller at each end to which the victim was fastened by the wrists and ankles, and had the joints of his limbs stretched by their rotation.

CHECK THE BOOK

Flamineo's reference at line 51 to 'the art of Wolner' is another example of the way Webster uses contemporary English references in the play. Wolner was a famous glutton who died from eating a raw eel; Falstaff calls him the 'singing man of Windsor' in Shakespeare's *Henry IV Part 2*. Flamineo is here commenting again on Francisco's exploitation of Marcello.

GLOSSARY

48	**early mushrooms** i.e. young upstarts, rising from lowly social origins
54	**screech-owl** name for the barn owl, regarded as a bird of ill omen from its harsh cry
58	**wind him** draw him out to discover his intentions
67	**stigmatic** condemned, branded, ugly
71	**raven** black bird of crow family also regarded as a bird of ill-omen
73	**crowner's** coroner's
81	**taffeta linings** silken underclothes
90	**girn** snarl, trap; referring to the setting of the face in a saucer of blood in the previous line
94	**strappadoed** a form of torture where the victim's hands were tied across his back and secured to a pulley; he was then hoisted from the ground and let down half way with a jerk
	felly or 'felloe': part of the rim of a wheel, supported by the spokes
96	**life of means deprives** deprives life of the means of making a living
117	**break** i.e. your covenant, become bankrupt
127	**Ud's death** by God's death

ACT IV

SCENE 1

- Francisco and Monticelso discuss Isabella's death.
- Monticelso urges Francisco to avenge it.
- Francisco borrows Monticelso's black book.
- Isabella's ghost appears to Francisco.
- He writes a love poem to Vittoria.

Monticelso encourages Francisco to reveal his thoughts and to accept that Isabella has been poisoned, urging him to avenge her death. Francisco does not want to fight because of the burden it would put on his people and argues that the initiator of the feud must bear the responsibility for all the evils it brings about (lines 5–11).

Monticelso suggests more insidious means as likely to prove more effective. He loans Francisco his 'black book' (line 33) which records the names and details of all the criminals and offenders in Rome. Francisco plans to use it to locate a list of murderers to kill Brachiano. He closes his eyes and calls Isabella to mind to help him decide how to avenge her death. Her ghost appears but Francisco thinks it is a figment of his imagination. He is inspired with an idea for revenge and dismisses the vision. He announces he is in love with Vittoria and writes her a poem which he sends to the house of convertites. He chooses Count Lodowick (Lodovico) as the right man to help avenge Isabella's death.

COMMENTARY

The scene exposes the thinking of Cardinal Monticelso and Francisco. Monticelso does not counsel prayer which would be appropriate to his position as a member of the clergy but revenge. His 'black book' (line 33) which records details of all the villains in Rome suggests the workings of the secret police in a tyrannical regime. Francisco is fascinated by it and his **ironic** comment is **satirical**: 'See the corrupted use some make of books' (line 94).

In most **revenge tragedies** it is the ghost who urges revenge. In this instance Francisco believes the appearance of Isabella's ghost to be simply a figment of his imagination. Nevertheless it does suggest a novel way for him to avenge her death – through a fiction. His announcement 'I am in love, / In love with Corombona…' (line 119) is confusing. It is only later that his motive in writing to her, to make Brachiano jealous and provoke him to abduct Vittoria from the house of convertites and marry her, becomes clear.

CHECK THE POEM

Monticelso argues that 'undermining more prevails / Than doth the cannon' (lines 13–14) meaning that a subtle form of revenge is likely to be more effective than open warfare. Satan uses the same argument in Milton's *Paradise Lost* when the devils discuss how to avenge themselves on God for banishing them from heaven: 'who overcomes / By force, hath overcome but half his foe' (I: 648–9).

CONTEXT

The 'black book' was originally an official record bound in black; it was later used to record the names of those liable to censure or punishment. Monticelso suggests that although it does not have magical powers, it contains the name of 'many devils' (lines 33–6). Hence the phrase 'to be in someone's black books', meaning to be out of favour.

CHECK THE BOOK

The reference to 'impudent bawds / That go in men's apparel' (lines 56–7) is a contemporary complaint by conservative authorities relating to the scandal of cross-dressing women, who were attacked in anti-feminist pamphlets such as *Hic Mulier* (1620) – the Latin masculine form of the pronoun is here used with the feminine noun to make the point about the inappropriateness of their behaviour.

CONTEXT

Francisco believes his vision of Isabella's ghost is caused by his 'melancholy' (line 100), that is an overproduction of black bile: one of the four humours in medieval and Renaissance physiology an imbalance of which was believed to be responsible for disease.

GLOSSARY

2   **loose ... hair** Virgin brides wore their hair loose at this time; a curious simile for a cleric which points forward to the wedding procession at the beginning of Act V

13   **undermining** military term, 'causing destruction by digging underneath fortifications'

15   **patient ... tortoise** the tortoise was regarded as an emblem of patience who defended itself by withdrawing into its shell

16   **with the lion** like the lion

28   **found** found out, discovered

39   **jealous** watchful, vigilant

41   **flax** linen, the fibres were used in wicks for candles

51   **taking up commodities** scam in which rather than charge illegally high rates of interest, swindlers loaned goods in place of money and then demanded repayment at an inflated price

      politic bankrupts those who hide their assets

52–5   **For ... children** Men who prostituted their wives and bought the silence of their friends

57–8   **usurers ... reportage** money lenders who bribed clerks for a recommendation

59   **antedate** predate

71   **tribute of wolves** King Edgar had ordered the Welsh to pay a tribute of three hundred wolves a year

80   **Irish ... heads** Elizabeth I's English army paid a ransom for heads in the Irish rebellions – they regarded the Irish as cruel and bloodthirsty (see line 136)

90   **leash** a set of three (a hunting term)

91   **laundress** furnish with laundresses (reputedly of easy virtue)

131   **When ... follow** i.e. mental powers are superior to physical

138   *Flectere ... movebo* 'If I cannot prevail on the gods above, I will move the infernal regions' (Virgil, *Aeneid* VII, 312); Acheron was the river of groaning in Hades (Hell)

SCENE 2

- Brachiano visits Vittoria in the house of convertites.
- He intercepts Francisco's love-letter and threatens to kill Vittoria.
- She is furious and defends herself.
- Brachiano plans to escape with Vittoria to Padua.

The Matron of the house of convertites is concerned that she will be held responsible for allowing Brachiano to visit Vittoria but Flamineo reassures her that the Pope is dying and the clergy have more important things to worry about. Francisco's servant arrives, sees Flamineo speaking to the Matron and asks her to deliver a letter. When Brachiano appears, Flamineo takes the letter and after a tussle with Brachiano, reads Francisco's letter aloud. In the letter, Francisco promises to rescue Vittoria and take her to Florence. Brachiano is distraught and at once believes that Vittoria has been unfaithful to him and threatens to destroy her (lines 40–2).

Brachiano is equally angry with Flamineo, who stands up for Vittoria. When the duke threatens him 'Would you be kicked?' Flamineo responds, 'Would you have your neck broke?' (line 52) reminding the duke and the audience of his role in Camillo's death. He tells the duke exactly what he thinks of him.

Vittoria enters and Brachiano confronts her with the letter. She realises that it is a trick but Brachiano instantly turns on her and asks, 'How long have I beheld the devil in crystal?' (line 86) – another reference to Vittoria as the 'devil' but **ironic** coming from Brachiano. He blames Vittoria for everything and tries to absolve himself of responsibility; likening himself to a 'heathen sacrifice' he accuses her of leading him to his 'eternal ruin', concluding with the reflection that 'Woman to man / Is either a god or a wolf' (lines 89–90). However, it is his self-pitying regret for his duchess

CHECK THE BOOK

In 'Why Should He Call Her Whore?' the first chapter of *Reading Shakespeare Historically* (Routledge, 1996) Lisa Jardine examines the importance attached to a woman's reputation and the number of cases of defamation which came before the Ecclesiastical Courts. She relates her research to Othello's accusation of Desdemona in Shakespeare's *Othello*.

CONTEXT

Bridewell in London was used as a house of correction for reformed prostitutes and for homeless children. Originally a royal residence built by Henry VIII, his son, Edward VI, gave it to the City of London.

Isabella's death, 'O my sweetest Duchess / How lovely art thou now?' (line 97) which rouses Vittoria's anger. She rejects his hypocritical, 'Whose death God pardon' (line 113) and points out both his responsibility and how much she has lost by her association with him: 'What have I gained by thee but infamy?' (line 105). She denounces both Brachiano and Flamineo; they attempt to soothe her but she rejects them furiously, vowing 'I'll speak not one word more' (line 188).

Eventually Brachiano embraces her and announces that he will pursue Francisco's plan to take Vittoria away, set out in the letter. He'll take her to Padua and marry her, making her his duchess. True to her word Vittoria does not speak throughout the rest of the scene while the men make plans. Flamineo relates a fable about a crocodile, a worm and a bird. He rejects the duke's obvious explanation and twists it to focus on Vittoria. In a final confidential aside he explains to the audience how he is playing the fool in order to advance himself: 'Knaves do grow great by being great men's apes' (line 243).

COMMENTARY

Vittoria is now a prisoner within the house of convertites. The majority of the scene, however, is like the Arraignment, taken up with Vittoria defending herself against charges of immorality – this time to her lover and brother. Her furious retort to the duke 'Whose death God revenge / On thee, most godless Duke' (lines 103–4) is one of many such lightly uttered curses which rebound on the subject.

The angry exchange between the duke and Flamineo is striking because Flamineo is normally so careful about not letting the duke know what he thinks; his disparaging comments are usually made in asides to the audience. Here, however, Flamineo pronounces his verdict to the duke's face: 'As in this world there are degrees of evils: / So in this world there are degrees of devils. / You're a great Duke; I your poor secretary' (lines 55–7). In this spine-tingling speech Flamineo spells out clearly his understanding of the duke as dangerous, corrupt and evil.

GLOSSARY

4	**Pope … deathbed** Gregory XIII, who was responsible for Vittoria's imprisonment, died in 1585
23	**conveyance** contrivance, underhand dealing; method of communication; document for transferring of property
25	**Your prop** meaning Brachiano; Vittoria is described as a vine needing the support of a man
28	**lees** dregs
33	**halter** noose
34	**willow** emblem of unrequited love
39	**atheists** the pagan gods in Francisco's letter can be defined as atheists – i.e. non-Christians
40	**atomies** atoms, small particles; anatomised, cut up bodies
45	**changeable stuff** material which changes according to the light, such as shot or watered silk, i.e. fickle woman
46–7	**O'er … wearing** in deep water therefore unfit for you – suggesting that she's weeping
49	**bloodhound** hunter for blood, one who seeks violence and sex
53	**Russia** Russians reportedly beat on the shins debtors who refused to pay
59	**Spanish fig** gesture of contempt; poisoned fig
	Italian sallet Italian salad (i.e. poisoned)
60	**ply your convoy** get on with conducting me
71	**characters** magical signs which cannot be understood
72	**receiver** pimp, procurer
73	**God's precious** by God's precious blood
75	**cabinet** casket
80	**reclaimed** tamed, reformed; plays on hawking term meaning 'calling back a hawk which has been allowed to fly'; 'bells' were attached to hawks' legs
81	**Ware hawk** beware of swindlers (slang), i.e. Vittoria
83	**lovely** attractive; amorous
86	**devil in crystal** been deceived; witches were said to see devils enclosed in a crystal
89–90	**Woman … wolf** proverbial, applied by Montaigne to marriage (*Essays*, translated by John Florio, III, v)
91	**adamants** loadstones or magnets which repel
94	**Irish funerals** in which professional mourners were hired to wail or keen

continued

CHECK THE POEM

The word 'will' in early modern English covered a variety of meanings including sexual senses of 'desire', 'penis', 'vagina'. In Sonnet 135 Shakespeare plays on these and his own name: 'Whoever hath her wish, thou hast thy "Will", / And "Will" to boot, and "Will" in overplus.'

CONTEXT

Flamineo makes a number of references to the famous classical stories, Homer's *Iliad* and his *Odyssey*. At lines 61–3, 'All … last', he is referring to the story in the *Odyssey* (IX, 369–70) in which the promise of Polyphemus, the Cyclops (a one-eyed giant), turned out to be to eat Ulysses (Odysseus) last of all. Eventually Ulysses blinds him and escapes.

CONTEXT

Flamineo is referring, at line 197, to the story of the wooden horse in Homer's *Iliad*. The Greeks had been besieging Troy for ten years demanding the return of the beautiful Helen of Troy, who had been abducted by the Trojan prince Paris. The Greeks built a huge wooden horse, which they left on the shore as a peace-offering before pretending to sail away. The idea of sexual intercourse inside the horse is Flamineo's own suggestion.

GLOSSARY

109	**Ill-scenting foxes** foxes, known for their foul smell, were thought to cure paralysis or palsy
115	**preferment** promotion
126	**Lethe** river of forgetfulness in Hades (Hell)
129	**poniards** daggers
146	**imposthume** festering sore
153	**mercer** merchant dealing in fine fabrics, especially silks
155	**frowardness** perversity, stubbornness
156	**leverets** young hares, mistresses
158	**full cry** full pursuit (by the hounds); weeping
159	**quat** squat (hunting term) crouching down like a cornered hare
162	**groats** coins worth four old pence
	broom-men street-sweepers
	use interest
164–5	**be ... blowing** blowing at a ferret forces it to let go of its prey
177–8	**great ... safely** a bridge such as London Bridge was impossible to pass underneath (shoot) at high tide, suggesting that Vittoria is dangerous in her anger
183	**good ... snowball** Brachiano's virtuous feelings increase now he no longer cares for her
187	**rewarded** hunting dogs and hawks were given part of the prey they helped to kill
200	**ingrateful Rome** the city was held to be ungrateful to its citizens
201	**Barbary** land of barbarians, the Saracen countries of north Africa
210–11	**Lay ... Padua** station relays of horses on the way, board ship and make all speed to Padua
214	**Florence** the duke of Florence

SCENE 3

- The Ambassadors process across the stage in preparation for the election of the new pope.
- Lodovico searches the cardinals' food for secret messages.
- Monticelso is elected Pope Paul IV.
- News arrives that Vittoria has fled to Padua with Brachiano, and Monticelso excommunicates them both.
- He questions Lodovico's motives; Lodovico 'confesses' and agrees to give up his vengeance.
- Francisco sends Lodovico a thousand ducats pretending they are from the Pope and Lodovico changes his mind again.

Francisco tells Lodovico to guard the conclave of cardinals gathered to elect a new pope. The Ambassadors appear dressed in ceremonial costume for the occasion. Lodovico checks the cardinals' dishes for secret messages. Monticelso's election as Pope Paul IV is announced.

Francisco learns to his joy that Vittoria and Brachiano have fled together, falling into his trap. Monticelso is pronouncing the papal blessing for the remission of sins when Francisco whispers news of Vittoria and Brachiano's flight. Monticelso's first act as pope is to excommunicate the couple.

All exit the stage except for Lodovico and Francisco, and the latter reminds Lodovico of his having 'ta'en the sacrament to prosecute / The intended murder' (line 73) of Brachiano – a blasphemous act. Lodovico expresses surprise that as a 'great prince' (line 76) Francisco plans to take part himself, but Francisco is determined to reap his revenge.

Monticelso returns and questions Lodovico as to Francisco's motives for begging pardon for him so passionately. He correctly surmises that Francisco plans to use Lodovico to commit murder. In a **parody** of the sacrament Lodovico 'confesses' to Monticelso who tells him the crime is damnable and he should repent. Monticelso's

CHECK THE BOOK

In the bare stages of the public theatres, costume provided a spectacular feast for the audience. In Act IV Scene 3 the Ambassadors pass over the stage in the ceremonial costume of their national orders.

CONTEXT

A 'conclave' (line 2) was the place in which cardinals met in secret to elect a new pope; the Sistine Chapel in Rome is still used for this purpose.

CONTEXT

Adultery was one of the sins which invoked automatic excommunication in the Catholic Church. In the middle ages a public ceremony was conducted which involved the tolling of a bell (as for the dead), the closing of the Book of the Gospels and snuffing out of a candle – hence the term 'to condemn with bell, book and candle'.

QUESTION

To what extent is Monticelso sincere in his counsel to Lodovico to repent?

argument is morally persuasive and Lodovico says he will give up the murderous plan. However, Francisco sends Lodovico a thousand crowns, which the servant tells him are from the Pope. He is then convinced that Monticelso was merely testing him and that the Pope secretly approves the plan to avenge Isabella's death.

COMMENTARY

A scene of splendour unfolds as the magnificently dressed Ambassadors process over the stage and Monticelso is elected Pope. It is **ironic** that we learn of the flight of Vittoria and Brachiano immediately after the announcement of Monticelso's election. His excommunication of the pair as his first act in his new office reveals the new pope, now clad in his white papal robes, as a hypocrite (see the end of Act II Scene 1 where Monticelso plots Brachiano's downfall with Francisco).

Lodovico's 'confession' is one of several Catholic sacraments which are blasphemously **parodied**. Monticelso's moral judgement on revenge is, however, theologically sound and morally persuasive. His question, 'Dost thou imagine thou canst slide on blood / And not be tainted with a shameful fall? (lines 119–20) might well sum up the play, indeed the whole of **revenge drama**.

GLOSSARY		
6	**several** various	
37	**scrutiny** technical term for the formal taking of individual votes	
38	**admiration** i.e. 'adoration' an alternative form of selection to the secret ballot in which two thirds of the cardinals turned towards a single candidate and bowed	
43–7	**_Denuntio ... Quartus_** (Latin) 'I announce to you tidings of great joy. The Most Reverend Cardinal Lorenzo de Monticelso has been elected to the Apostolic See, and has chosen for himself the name of Paul IV. ALL: Long Live the Holy Father Paul IV.' (The historical Cardinal Montalto became Pope Sixtus V)	
58–9	**The ... wrong** i.e. deeds must follow passionate words	
60–1	**_Concedimus ... peccatorum_** (Latin) 'We grant you the Apostolic blessing and remission of sins'	

GLOSSARY

73	**sacrament** one of seven Christian ceremonies in Catholicism
83	**resolve** show
87	**out of measure** excessively
94	**resty** restive, uncontrollable
	Barbary horse small horse from the Barbary coast; a barb
95–6	**career … ring-galliard** technical exercises in the management of horses
97	**French rider** the French were renowned for horsemanship and sexual expertise
130	**suffrage** intercessory prayers; support
142	**told** counted
146	**puling** sickly
150	**sounds … plummet** measures my intentions with gold, as a (lead) plumbline is used to test depth

CHECK THE BOOK

Obviously inspired by the image of the glow-worm as a **simile** for the transience of human glory and the deceiving nature of appearance which he found in Alexander's *Alexandrean Tragedy*, Webster re-uses lines 41–2 of this scene in *The Duchess of Malfi*.

ACT V

SCENE 1

- The wedding procession of Vittoria and Brachiano crosses the stage.
- Brachiano welcomes the disguised Francisco as the moor Mulinassar.
- The conspirators discuss plans to murder Brachiano.
- Cornelia and Marcello object to Flamineo's relationship with Zanche; Cornelia strikes and Marcello kicks her.
- Flamineo accuses Marcello of possessing a hot temper (choler) and suggests that he is not really their father's son. Marcello challenges him to a duel.
- Zanche confesses her love to Mulinassar (Francisco).

There is a silent passage across the stage of Brachiano, Flamineo, Vittoria, Marcello, Hortensio, Cornelia, Zanche and others. Although it is never explicitly stated, this must be the wedding

CHECK THE BOOK

'Marriages were festive as well as sacred occasions … Whereas the ecclesiastical solemnisation took place in a matter of minutes, the nuptial cheer could go on for hours or even days' (David Cressy, *Birth, Marriage & Death: Ritual, Religion, and the Life-cycle in Tudor and Stuart England*, Oxford University Press, 1997, p. 350).

procession of Brachiano and Vittoria. Flamineo confides that he is 'happy' (line 3) for the first time in his life. This in itself is probably a warning that things are going to start to go wrong and the immediate introduction of a stranger should alert the audience. Flamineo and Hortensio discuss 'the Moor that's come to court' (line 4). The audience are not yet aware that it is Francisco in disguise, especially as it was common for actors to double parts. Flamineo praises him – 'I have not seen a goodlier personage' (line 6). Praise of anyone is so unlike Flamineo that it suggests that his normally suspicious mind has been lulled into a false sense of security.

Flamineo and Hortensio, one of his officers, go on to discuss the Hungarian noblemen soldiers (Lodovico, Antonelli and Gasparo also in disguise) who have become Capuchin monks and sleep in their armour. Brachiano welcomes the newcomers and awards Mulinassar a 'competent pension' (line 47) (a salary of an adequate amount) and invites them all to stay for the 'barriers' (line 56), the celebratory tournament in honour of his marriage.

The disguised conspirators (Francisco, Lodovico, Antonelli, Gasparo, Pedro, Carlo, Fernese) discuss how to murder Brachiano. 'Carlo and Pedro' (s.d. line 43) may be the names taken by Lodovico and Gasparo in disguise or the treacherous members of Brachiano's court who are indeed of Francisco's faction as he boasted at IV.3.77–8. Most editors assume the latter and include them as separate characters. Lodovico, who prides himself on his artistry (for example in Act I Scene 1 he talks about taking revenge in terms of 'Italian cutworks'), wants something original that will make them famous – poison preferably in some situation where Brachiano will curse and hence go straight to hell (lines 75–7). Francisco argues that though there's no swifter means of revenge than that decided upon, he would have preferred to fight Brachiano on the battlefield and after 'Led him to Florence!' (line 82). If they did not before, the audience must now guess who Mulinassar is.

Marcello comments on the fact that Zanche has become attached to Flamineo, and chides him for it: 'Why doth this devil haunt you?' (line 86). Flamineo and Marcello discuss military affairs with Francisco. He refuses to discuss his service on account of his modesty. They talk about the hard life of soldiers and the 'misery of peace' (line 116). Flamineo advises Francisco to get Brachiano's promise of a pension in writing while the courtiers prepare for the barriers.

Flamineo discusses Zanche with Hortensio, saying that he loves her 'as a man holds a wolf by the ears. But for fear of turning upon me, and pulling out my throat, I would let her go to the devil' (lines 153–5). She accuses him of no longer loving her 'your love to me rather cools than heats' (line 161) as he tries to convince her she is wrong.

Cornelia enters and insults Zanche, telling her to go to the 'stews' (line 185), that is the brothels in the red-light district. Flamineo reprimands his mother, reminding her that it is prohibited to strike at court. When Zanche answers Cornelia back Marcello kicks her and calls her 'strumpet' (line 189). Flamineo objects to this treatment but Marcello says 'She brags that you shall marry her' (line 193) and continues to insult Zanche – he'd rather she were a scarecrow used to frighten 'Her fellow crows' (line 196). Flamineo retorts by accusing his brother of being 'choleric' (line 200) and says that he suspects 'my mother played foul play / When she conceived thee' (lines 203–4). At this imputation of bastardy Marcello is furious and swears that he will challenge his brother to a duel: 'Those words I'll make thee answer / With thy heart blood' (lines 207–8). Flamineo taunts his brother but accepts, 'You know where you shall find me—' (line 209).

The scene concludes with Zanche unexpectedly telling Mulinassar (Francisco) that she loves him. He responds that he is old now and has vowed never to marry. But Zanche says she can provide a rich dowry and furthermore can tell him things that 'shall startle your blood' (line 228).

COMMENTARY

This scene again opens with a magnificent spectacle as the bridal procession crosses the stage. Vittoria would be gorgeously dressed with her hair loose and flowing and sprinkled with white orris powder (see the **Detailed Summary** for Act V Scene 3). The Ambassadors, still in their costumes from the previous scene, are most likely present – although not mentioned specifically most editors and directors assume they are part of the opening stage

> **CONTEXT**
>
> 'Goose' (line 208) was a common term for a prostitute and from the middle ages prostitutes plying their trade in the Southwark stews were known as 'Winchester geese' since the land around the then palace of the Bishop of Winchester, now roughly where Southwark Cathedral is, belonged to the see of Winchester and was exempt from the city's strict regulation. The suburbs were the largest growing areas of the capital and were notorious as haunts of rogues and vagabonds, thieves and prostitutes. They were also the location for entertainments such as bear-baiting and theatres like the Rose and the Globe.

direction '*and others*'. This may seem surprising given that the Church has excommunicated the pair and Vittoria is a proclaimed whore, but their presence underlines the play's **satirical** view of the power of the great and the sycophancy of those hoping to ingratiate themselves and profit from them. Cornelia and Marcello, Vittoria's mother and her other brother, are also present despite their condemnation of her relationship with Brachiano.

This scene marks the play's turning point and the audience will be only too aware that everything is about to change. Up to this point we have followed Flamineo's fortunes; for better or worse, he has been the one in charge of all the schemes and plots. Now suddenly, at the point when he seems to have achieved the status and success he so desired, he is no longer making the running. Others are hatching plots which threaten to undo everything he thinks he has gained.

The soldiers' debate about their military careers allows for some wonderfully ironic lines, and raises one of the fundamental questions of the play – what accounts for the differences between people? Can it simply be determined by an individual's place in the social structure? Francisco says he will not flatter the duke:

> What difference is between the duke and I? No more than between two bricks; all made of one clay. Only't may be one is placed on the top of the turret; the other in the bottom of a well by mere chance; (lines 106–111)

Francisco's answer that social standing is simply a question of chance is obviously what Flamineo wants to hear, since it flatters his belief that it is only through the perversity of fortune that he is not a duke. It is doubly ironic, though, since Francisco is, in fact, a duke himself. At another level it suggests that Francisco is at least as clever and sophisticated as Flamineo.

The attitude of Marcello and Cornelia towards Zanche is disturbing. Up to now they have seemed to represent a proper moral perspective within the play in their condemnation of the relationship between Vittoria and Brachiano. It was perhaps surprising then to find them at their wedding but the audience may

---

CONTEXT

One way in which Webster signals that a turning-point has been reached is that Flamineo starts to lose his superb linguistic control and now becomes the victim rather than the perpetrator of the play's **irony**; for example at line 10 when he mentions 'Candy' i.e. Crete. At II.1.290 we saw how the island which was famous for poisoned snakes, had become a **metaphor** for death but at this point Flamineo fails to spot the pun.

understand this in terms of family loyalty, accepting the situation and making the best of it. Their dislike of and violence towards Zanche seems largely based on her colour – she is also a Moor. Zanche's sudden confession of love for Mulinassar is disconcerting, but given other characters' attitudes (even Flamineo calls her 'gipsy', line 161) it is not surprising that she might feel affection for one she believes to be her countryman. It is ironic, of course, that it is really Francisco in disguise.

GLOSSARY

16	**Capuchins** Franciscans: friars in the reformed order of St Francis, named after the sharp-pointed hood or *'capuche'* they wore (which offer a useful disguise for Lodovico and Gasparo)
26	**coats of mail** monks often did penance by wearing a 'hair shirt' next to their skin so a coat of mail would indeed be 'hard penance'
47	**inly sorry** inwardly grieved
57	**private standings** special places reserved for you to see the entertainments from
62	**presence** the presence chamber, a room for giving audience to the court
72	**hazard** in 'real' tennis (from which the modern game is derived), 'each of the winning openings in a tennis court'
89	**one up** Flamineo shifts the sense to refer to his erection which must be laid down through his mistress's 'cunning', i.e. magic, art, with sexual innuendo
120	**Colossuses** referring to the Colossus of Rhodes, the huge statue of the sun-god at the harbour entrance
122	**arras** hanging tapestries which allowed for concealment
127–9	**pigeons ... Manor** a common complaint and a metaphor for social inequality; pigeons were domesticated and bred for food for the aristocracy
	Fowling-piece shotgun
134	**under his hand** in writing
148	**almanacs** books of tables which claimed to fortell the future but were notoriously unreliable
152	**constrainedly** of necessity, under compulsion

continued

www. CHECK THE NET
Francisco disguises himself as the Moor, Mulinassar, in order to enter Brachiano's service and avenge Isabella's death. The term Moor was often used as a religious designation, meaning Muslim, however, like Othello in Shakespeare's play, Mulinassar claims to be a Christian. A Moorish Ambassador to Elizabeth's court was resident in London for six months in 1600–1 and may have been the model for Othello and Mulinassar. His portrait may be found at: **http://www.rsc.org. uk.** Search for Shakespeare's Moors' and click directly over picture to enlarge it.

CONTEXT

Many words have changed meaning since Webster was writing, hence the need for a glossary to explain what they originally meant. The way in which many words are pronounced has also changed over time so that many puns and a lot of wordplay is missed. For example, it is thought that 'satin' (line 166) was spoken in such a way that it sounded like 'Satan'. Such wordplay is designed to provide a moral commentary on the text.

GLOSSARY

161 **gipsy** referring to her dark skin: gipsies were thought to come from Egypt; contemptuous term for a woman; cunning rogue

180–1 **shoemakers ... bacon** salt bacon draws men on to drink as shoemakers draw shoes on to feet

185 **haggard** wild female hawk or (contemptuously) woman

186 **clapped ... heels** put in irons or the stocks

strike ... court a punishable offence

188 **bedstaff** used in supporting or making up a bed

191–2 **walnut-tree ... fruit** refers to the proverb: 'A woman, a dog, and a walnut tree / The more you beat them the better they be'

199 **fan of feathers** one that a courtier would hold

201 **rhubarb** was used as a purgative

211 **him** i.e. Flamineo

216 **Michaelmas** 29 September when an 'Indian summer' is possible; Francisco is suggesting that he is too old for Zanche

223 **presentment** presentation, gift

SCENE 2

- Cornelia interrogates Marcello.
- Flamineo runs Marcello through with his own sword, killing him.
- Lodovico sprinkles Brachiano's 'beaver' (face-guard of a helmet) with poison.

Cornelia says that she has heard rumours that Marcello is to fight and she wants to know with whom. He denies it and then asks her about his crucifix, whether it was his father's and recalling how whilst she suckled Flamineo as a baby he broke a section of it off.

Flamineo enters announcing 'I have brought your weapon back' (line 14) before running Marcello through with it. Marcello dies, believing that his death is divine retribution for their sins on the whole family. With his dying breath he makes a moral reflection on the dangers of ambition (lines 20–4).

Cornelia is distraught, 'O my perpetual sorrow!' (line 25). Hortensio, Carlo and Pedro help carry her away from the body. She asks for a 'looking-glass' or 'some feathers' (lines 38–40) to see whether Marcello is still breathing, in a passage which clearly recalls King Lear's grief at the death of Cordelia. Brachiano returns with Flamineo and asks him if this was his 'handiwork'. Flamineo responds 'It was my misfortune' (line 47), which invites questions once more as to what constitutes 'fortune' and the extent to which individuals shape their own destiny.

Cornelia denies that Flamineo is responsible, arguing that those who prevented Marcello receiving better help are the guilty ones. She then runs at Flamineo with her knife but cannot bring herself to strike and lets it fall. Brachiano demands to know what happened but Cornelia covers up for her son and blames Marcello for starting it. The Page denies her version of events but Cornelia says that as she has lost one son she does not wish to lose another.

Brachiano orders the body to be taken to Cornelia's lodging and that no one should tell Vittoria. He refuses to pardon Flamineo, saying that he will rather give Flamineo a daily reprieve to be renewed each evening. This is his revenge for Flamineo having 'braved' him, that is stood up to him once, referring to the occasion in the house of convertites (Act IV Scene 2). While all this is happening Lodovico sprinkles Brachiano's beaver with poison. Brachiano calls for it in order to start the fencing and Francisco comments in an **aside** full of **irony**: 'This shall his passage to the black lake further, / The last good deed he did, he pardoned murder' (lines 83–4).

COMMENTARY

The audience have been prepared for the tournament and will be expecting the conspirators to attempt to kill Brachiano. The duel between Flamineo and Marcello has seemed relatively insignificant and it is shocking that Flamineo, with no warning, simply runs his brother through. The story of Flamineo as a baby breaking off part of a crucifix is an ill omen and suggests innate evil. It is not clear if

---

CONTEXT

Marcello likens himself and Flamineo to the sons of Oedipus (V.1.205), Eteocles and Polynices, who killed each other fighting for their father's throne; it was said that the flames of their joint funeral pyre parted, suggesting that their enmity continued after death.

CHECK THE BOOK

Shakespeare uses the same **metaphor** as Webster does at lines 69–70 of shooting a second arrow in the hope of finding the first in *The Merchant of Venice* when Bassanio asks Antonio to lend him the money to go to Belmont to woo the rich heiress Portia: 'In my schooldays, when I had lost one shaft, / I shot his fellow of the selfsame flight' (I.1.142–6).

CHECK THE BOOK

The ghost of Hamlet's father appears to Horatio, Barnardo and Marcellus in 'the very armour he had on' when he fought the king of Norway. When Hamlet questions how then he could be recognised Horatio answers, 'my lord, he wore his beaver up'.

CONTEXT

Staged tournaments, such as the 'barriers' to celebrate Brachiano and Vittoria's wedding, were a popular form of entertainment in the royal court. Medieval chivalry and the chivalric orders now fulfilled purely symbolic public and political roles rather than the military functions for which they were instituted.

this is what Marcello is referring to in his dying reflections that, 'There are some sins which heaven doth duly punish / In a whole family' (lines 20–1). His final remark recalls Vittoria's dream to the audience's mind and seems designed to suit Brachiano's case, 'That tree shall long time keep a steady foot / Whose branches spread no wider than the root' (lines 23–4). This is a proverbial warning against overweening ambition. Marcello's speech seems to play across notions of divine justice and the biblical saying that the sins of the father should be visited upon the children (Exodus 20:5, Deuteronomy 5:9) but also articulates the idea that individuals are responsible for their own destinies by the conduct of their lives.

Brachiano is unwilling, or cannot, punish Flamineo, perhaps because Flamineo knows too much and is too close to him. Brachiano does not want Vittoria to be told and, significantly, he does not stop his own wedding celebrations from going ahead, which implies both a casual attitude to death and a failure of sympathy and understanding. These characteristics are not unexpected, however, from the man who calmly ordered his wife's death and enjoyed watching it. It is against these shocking events that Lodovico sprinkles poison on Brachiano's beaver. No words are spoken, which recalls the **dumb show** in which Brachiano witnessed the preparations for Isabella's death. It is appropriate that it should be his beaver that is poisoned since it approximates most closely to the place where Isabella was tainted on the lips.

GLOSSARY

8	**Publish** make public
16	**sanctuary** church where he cannot be arrested
32–3	**rear up's head** hold his head up
63–7	**indeed … bosom** Cornelia is lying to save Flamineo's life by claiming that Marcello drew first
69	**grazed** either referring to Marcello's wound or 'grassed' meaning 'lost in the grass'
83	**black lake** probably Acherusia in Hades (Hell)

SCENE 3

- Brachiano is poisoned.
- Lodovico and Gasparo, disguised as Capuchins, strangle him.
- Zanche tells Francisco how Isabella and Camillo were killed and plans to flee with him.

The ceremonial martial exercises (fighting at the 'barriers') commence. Brachiano calls for an armourer and removes his beaver, realising that he has been poisoned. He has the armourer arrested and sent off to be tortured to make him confess and Flamineo sends for doctors.

Brachiano realises he is going to die. Giovanni is upset, 'O my most loved father!' (line 16), but is taken away and Brachiano calls for Vittoria, 'Where's this good woman?' (line 17). His words at this point demonstrate his love: 'Had I infinite worlds / They were too little for thee' (lines 18–19). But he says 'Do not kiss me, for I shall poison thee' (line 28), recognising the duke of Florence as responsible for his death. Brachiano then compares 'soft natural death' (line 30) to the harsher fate attending the death of 'princes' (line 35) (those of noble birth such as he). He is angry, even with Vittoria 'How miserable a thing it is to die, / 'Mongst women howling' (lines 36–7) and departs into his private apartment.

Flamineo reflects on the fate of 'dying princes' (line 43) **ironically** with the disguised Francisco, the prince who is himself responsible for Brachiano's death. Lodovico (also still disguised) says that, although Brachiano's wits are becoming confused, he has made Vittoria his heir until Giovanni comes of age, which Flamineo regards as 'good luck' (line 82).

Brachiano re-enters, distressed and speaking incoherently, accusing those around him and seeing terrifying visions. His talk becomes disjointed as he flits from one idea to another, but the visions he sees as he starts to lose his wits are painfully apt. He sees a devil, for example, and he sees Flamineo 'dancing on the ropes there: and he

CONTEXT

Flamineo's reference to the 'compass o'th'verge' (line 55) relates to the area within a twelve-mile radius of the king's court, subject to the jurisdiction of the Lord High Steward and signified by the rod or wand he carried as an emblem of authority or symbol of office. It suggests a bawdy pun on the primary meaning of 'verge' as 'penis'.

CONTEXT

It was traditional to sprinkle fragrant white powdered orris root (*Iris germanica* often considered a herb of Venus, the goddess of love) on to a bride's loose hair. In his disintegrating mental state Brachiano points out that it makes Vittoria look as though she's had sex in the pastry room and got covered in flour ('hair … pastry', lines 119–20).

CONTEXT

This passage on the death of Brachiano (lines 137–48) is based on the *Funus* of Erasmus, a satirical account of the deaths of a good Christian in comparison with the wealthy and corrupt Georgius Balearicus.

carries / A money-bag in each hand, to keep him even, / For fear of breaking's neck' (lines 112–114). He sees Vittoria with her hair powdered for the wedding and laughs at her appearance. He points to Lodovico and Gasparo, disguised as monks and advises that they should avoid churchmen and likens them to rats. He claims 'I'll do a miracle: I'll free the court from all foul vermin' (lines 127–8) and calls for Flamineo. Flamineo sees this as an ill omen (lines 129–31).

Brachiano seems near death and Lodovico and Gasparo as monks prepare for it by reciting Latin prayers over his body. They send the rest away and in a **parody** of the *Commendatio animae* (religious service in which the souls of the dead are commended to God) they reveal their true identities and commend his soul not to God but the devil, reciting all his sins. When Brachiano calls Vittoria they strangle him to prevent discovery, joking that the cord they use is 'a true-love knot / Sent from the Duke of Florence' (lines 176–7). They congratulate themselves on the deed, convinced that no one could have 'done't quaintlier' (line 180).

Vittoria is distraught at Brachiano's death, 'O me! This place is hell' (line 181). Flamineo is cynical about her grief and is only concerned that the duke has left him nothing. Francisco (still in disguise) ironically comments, 'Sure, this was Florence' doing' to which Flamineo assents admiringly (lines 192–9). Francisco suggests that now people will be free to speak ill of Brachiano but Flamineo retorts that such critics would be hypocrites since princes only do what anyone would if they had their power.

Francisco praises Lodovico and asks for details of Brachiano's death but at Zanche's entrance, Lodovico says he will have to wait. Francisco feigns grief at Brachiano's death but Zanche ironically tells Francisco that he has no cause to weep, only the guilty parties need do so. She goes on to relate a dream from which she claims she knew that something evil would happen but that it mainly concerned him. Francisco pretends that he, too, had a dream about her. She is flattered and tells him how Isabella and Camillo died. She confesses she knew of it and intends, out of contrition, to rob Vittoria that night and escape with him, arranging to meet him at the chapel at midnight.

COMMENTARY

This is a shocking scene which starts with the ceremonial display of violence of the barriers, representing the idealised chivalric values of a past age. The audience, however, know that it is only a matter of time before the poison will start to work and Brachiano will die. As with Marcello at his death, Brachiano's words play across different ways of understanding the meaning of his life and death, corresponding to different literary genres. At one level Brachiano knows that Francisco is responsible and that he is the victim of a **revenge tragedy**; at another he sees himself as a victim of Fate as in a *de casibus* tragedy (that is a medieval tragedy relating the fall of great men based on Boccaccio's *De Casibus Virorum Illustribus* 1355–60) – hence he addresses himself to Death: 'Most politic hangman!' (line 22).

Francisco's language in his conversation with Flamineo is interesting, too, as it reveals his far greater powers of discretion and cunning. He speaks simple conventional words appropriate to the situation, all the time drawing Flamineo out: 'How mean you?' and 'What did'st thou think of him? 'Faith speak freely' (lines 53 and 61).

Despite its tragic nature, there is an uncomfortable amount of humour in the scene which has a disturbing effect. As Flamineo says, 'the rare tricks of the Machiavellian' (line 195) will make you 'die laughing' (line 198). His comment when Brachiano repeats his name is prescient: 'I do not like that he names me so often, / Especially on's death-bed: 'tis a sign I shall not live long' (lines 129–31). Flamineo's claim that he is willing to speak with Brachiano again, despite the presence of 'forty devils' (line 211), suggests a sort of casual desperation. Zanche and Francisco's meeting reminds the audience of Vittoria's meeting with Brachiano in Act I Scene 2 and her relating a dream which led to murder. Lodovico's sexist commentary on their encounter is reminiscent of Flamineo's with an added racist element.

CONTEXT

Elizabeth I and James I both raised money for the Crown by the grant of **'monopolies'** (line 73) allowing certain individuals exclusive rights or control of the trade in a commodity, product or service. For example Sir Walter Ralegh was granted the monopoly controlling cloth exports from London and, in 1584, a similar monopoly of wines, which made him a very wealthy man. The system was a cause of contention between the Crown and parliament.

CHECK THE BOOK

The White Devil contains many references to witches and witchcraft, such as Brachiano's at lines 124–5 where the grey rats he claims to see are most likely a reference to witches who supposedly turned themselves into animals without tails. For a fuller discussion of witchcraft in the play see Muriel West's *The Devil and John Webster* (University of Salzburg, 1974).

CONTEXT

The reference at lines 185–6 about wishing 'more rivers to the city' is another contemporary London reference to Sir Hugh Myddelton's artificial new river which was started in 1608 and supplied water to the capital.

GLOSSARY	
21–3	**Most ... friends** Brachiano addresses Death as a scheming murderer killing arbitrarily
28	**unction** ointment
57	**wolf** ulcerous sore
58	**poultry** puns on 'paltry' refuse, rubbish
85	**conveyed ... territories** exported money, a serious offence
93	**quails** small birds, a delicacy (wrongly believed to feed on poison) prostitutes
94	**dog-fish** small shark, used contemptuously of people
95	**dog-fox** male fox, renowned for cunning
101	**cod-piece** front flap or pouch that attaches to the front of the crotch of men's trousers to provide a covering for the genitals, often elaborately decorated; no longer fashionable by 1612
115	**whipt** trimmed
116	**cuts capers** makes frolicsome leaps, dances madly; to 'cut a caper on nothing' meant 'to be hanged'
132	*Attende ... Brachiane* the beginning of a Latin prayer the *Commendatio Animae*, the commending of the soul to God
137–48	*Domine ... laevum* i.e. 'LODOVICO: Lord Brachiano, you were accustomed to be guarded in battle by your shield; now this shield [i.e. the crucifix] you shall oppose against your infernal enemy.— GASPARO: once with your spear you prevailed in battle; now this holy spear [i.e. the holy taper] you shall wield against the enemy of souls.— LODOVICO: Listen, lord Brachiano, if you now also approve what has been done between us, turn your head to the right.— GASPARO: Rest assured, Lord Brachiano, think how many good deeds you have done – lastly remember that my soul is pledged for yours if there should be any peril.— LODOVICO: If you now also approve what has been done between us, turn your head to the left'
163	**winter plague** i.e. a virulent strain since the plague commonly occurred in summer
178	**snuff** burning candle-end, a metaphor for 'life' but also means 'what is weak or feeble' and 'fit of rage'
	woman-keeper female nurse, often believed to kill off patients
179	**pest-house** hospital for plague victims built in the city of London in 1594

GLOSSARY

184	**dispend** expend
187	**moonish** changeable (like the moon)
199	**saffron** spice, a stimulant taken in moderation but fatal in excess
207	**thresher** one who separates grain from straw by beating with a flail; one who thrashes or beats another; sea-fox or fox-shark
235	**Irish mantle** blanket worn by Irish peasants with no other clothes
250	**bed nest is broke** the mystery is explained
255	**usurers** money-lenders
263–4	**wash ... white** from the biblical proverb 'Can the Ethiope change his skin, or the leopard his spots?' (Jeremiah 13:23)
270–2	**partridge ... shame** i.e. the end justifies the means; puns on idea that partridges ate laurel (symbol of fame or victory) as a purge

SCENE 4

- Giovanni overhears Flamineo making insulting remarks about him and forbids his presence.
- Cornelia becomes mad with grief.
- She prepares Marcello's body for burial.
- Brachiano's ghost appears to Flamineo.
- Flamineo resolves to ask Vittoria what reward she intends to give him for his service and to kill her if she refuses.

Flamineo and Gasparo discuss Giovanni, who is now the new duke following his father's death. Flamineo disagrees with Gasparo's positive view of him but adds that he would not say so to his face, 'This is behind him. Now to his face—all comparisons were hateful' (line 3). Giovanni overhears and tells Flamineo to leave but Flamineo replies insolently that it is he who has cause to grieve rather than Giovanni since Giovanni is now duke. Giovanni dismisses him, telling him to pray and 'be penitent' (line 20). This

CHECK THE BOOK

Lines 159–60 'broke ... poisoned' contain a reference to the death of Amy Robsart, the wife of Elizabeth I's favourite Robert Dudley, Earl of Leicester. Dudley was ambitious and many believed that he had arranged his wife's death in order to be free to marry Elizabeth. An investigating jury found no evidence to substantiate this but rumours of his involvement haunted him for the rest of his life.

CHECK THE BOOK

Webster reuses Giovanni's lines 21–2 almost exactly in his next tragedy *The Duchess of Malfi*: 'I suffer now for what has former bin / Sorrow is held the eldest child of sin' (V.5.53–4).

rebuke from a young man disturbs Flamineo who feels himself losing his grip (lines 23–4) but he says he does not care and that Giovanni already resembles Francisco in miniature (lines 29–30).

A courtier tells Flamineo that Giovanni has forbidden him to enter the presence-chamber or any of his private rooms. Flamineo jokes but privately threatens revenge. Francisco tells him that his mother, Cornelia, 'Is grown a very old woman in two hours' (line 52). She is preparing Marcello's corpse for burial, weeping, singing sad songs and distributing flowers, distracted by grief. When Zanche tells her it is Flamineo she does not believe her, takes his hand and asks 'Can blood so soon be washed out?' (line 81). Cornelia sings a dirge for her dead son, 'Call for the robin-red-breast and the wren' (line 92). Finally even Flamineo is moved to pity her (lines 110–12). He resolves to ask Vittoria for recompense for his service to the duke.

Brachiano's ghost appears, throws earth at Flamineo and shows him a skull. The ghost's appearance makes Flamineo reckless and he resolves to kill Vittoria if she will not reward him.

COMMENTARY

At the beginning of Act V Flamineo was congratulating himself on how finally everything was going right for him. Shortly afterwards he kills his brother; then Brachiano dies and now he is forbidden even to come into the presence of Giovanni, the new young duke. Finally Brachiano's ghost appears to him. In fact he says 'I am falling to pieces already' (lines 23–4). There is a terrible sense of the inevitability of his doom in his recklessness and despair. The only person left he can turn to is his sister but he vows to kill her if she fails to give him what he wants.

The more the audience see of Flamineo the more they understand his egocentricity, self-absorption and his folly. He is too clever by half, can never keep his mouth shut and unwisely voices his thoughts about Giovanni and is overheard. Flamineo compounds this by pointing out how Giovanni has benefited from his father's death so it is hardly surprising he is forbidden his presence. On the other hand it may be that his analysis of Giovanni's character is accurate. Even at his most cynical and contemptuous, Flamineo's

CONTEXT

The drawing back of the *'traverse'* (the curtain at the back of the stage, line 62) to reveal Cornelia and the other women *'winding* Marcello's *corse'* (corpse) presents a tableau of powerful visual significance. It may well remind spectators of King Lear's cradling of Cordelia at the end of Shakespeare's play but that itself is a visual reminder of the *pietà* that is the image of Mary the mother of Christ cradling his body after the crucifixion.

description of the court has proved accurate, so that we are bound to consider whether these comments about Giovanni – that he is equally vicious and tyrannical and will reveal his nature in time – are also true. As so often Flamineo couches his remarks in terms of an animal fable, this time concerning a 'peacock' and an 'eagle'. Giovanni, he claims, will eventually reveal his true nature, 'his long tallants ... will grow out in time' (lines 6–9); when this is analysed in detail Flamineo revealingly appears to identify himself with the 'courtly peacock', suggesting superficiality, external magnificence but also an ostentatious, proud, or vain person.

Flamineo though is moved by the sight of his mother's madness and for the first time he confesses to a sense of his own wrong-doing and the stirrings of conscience: 'I have lived / Riotously ill ... And sometimes, when my face was full of smiles / Have felt the maze of conscience in my breast' (lines 115–18). It is this capacity for insight, even a potential for good within Flamineo, which finally makes him a tragic figure, since the audience see that he is a man who has taken the wrong path in his life but who, despite all, has the capacity for redemption. This scene is full of echoes of two of Shakespeare's best-known tragedies. Cornelia's madness is clearly modelled on Ophelia's in *Hamlet*. Not recognising Flamineo she distributes flowers in a scene reminiscent of Ophelia's madness after the death of her father, 'There's rosemary for you and rue for you / Heart's ease for you' (lines 75–6). The appearance of Brachiano as a ghost and holding a skull also seems to come from *Hamlet*, whereas the reference to her hand and the washing of blood from it is reminiscent of Lady Macbeth's sleepwalking scene in *Macbeth*.

CHECK THE BOOK

Flamineo's awakening of conscience is echoed in Book IV of Milton's *Paradise Lost* when Satan debates with himself, 'now conscience wakes despair / That slumbered, wakes the bitter memory / Of what he was'.

CONTEXT

The appearance of Brachiano's ghost is emblematic: the 'leather cassock' (long coat often worn by soldiers) was customary for a stage ghost. Burial in a friar's cowl was supposed to bring remission of sins, and the 'pot of lily-flowers' (white or Madonna lilies) signifies purity but in conjunction with the skull denotes 'Vice'.

GLOSSARY	
6	**dottrels** species of plover, notoriously easy to catch, hence 'fools', 'simpletons'
12	**wot** know
28	**cullis** strong broth – in this case made from chicken bones and gold (believed to have medicinal qualities)
30	***decimo-sexto*** small book (in which each page is one sixteenth of a full sheet); very small person

continued

CONTEXT

Webster has confused the Scythian philosopher 'Anacharsis' (line 25), who was renowned for wisdom, with Anaxarchus who was 'pounded to death in a mortar' for speaking contemptuously of the tyrant Nicocreon. He was famous for 'jesting at death'.

CHECK THE NET

The 'Castle Angelo' (line 39) is a reference to the Castel Sant'Angelo in Rome where the real-life Vittoria was imprisoned for a time, while the 'tower yonder' (line 40) suggests the Tower of London (near the theatre) in which King James I had his cousin Arbella Stewart imprisoned when she married without his permission. She was not politically ambitious and never pressed her claim to the English throne. Go to **www. elizabethan-era.org.uk** and click on 'Elizabethan Times' for details of her life.

GLOSSARY

35	**office** duty
45–6	**flaming firebrand** a piece of wood kindled at the fire; one who is doomed or deserves to burn in hell; one who kindles strife or mischief – Flamineo is playing on his own name
47	**smoor** smother, put out, i.e. kill
62	**traverse** curtain drawn across the back of the stage
64	**rosemary** fragrant evergreen shrub, a symbol of immortality and remembrance and thus customary at weddings and funerals
66–8	**bays ... lightning** laurel or bay wreaths were reputed to protect from lightning
75	**rue** evergreen shrub with bitter, strong-scented leaves; sorrow, regret
76	**heart's-ease** pansy associated with tranquillity
82–5	**When ... hear** popular superstitions believed to signify imminent death
86	**speckled** a sign of sin
91	**and** if
92	**robin-red-breast ... wren** birds believed to cover and tend dead bodies; wrens were believed to be female robins
96	**dole** rites, sorrow
97–101	**ant ... again** popular superstitions regarding beneficial creatures but the wolf was seen as an instrument of God's revenge, a supposed sign of death by murder
119	**Oft ... try** i.e. either 'Those who wear such clothes (courtiers) experience the tortures of conscience', or 'Those tortures torment those who wear such clothes'
123–4	**starry ... dungeon** heaven or hell but also signifying parts of the theatre, the 'gallery' above and the 'trapdoor' below
130	**shadows** feeble creatures; hangers-on; delusions; actors – compare *Macbeth* 'Life's but a walking shadow'
136	**familiars** i.e. friends still on earth
139	**beyond melancholy** despair, the next stage in derangement after melancholy

SCENE 5

- Lodovico persuades Francisco to leave the court, and the conclusion of their revenge on Brachiano to him.
- Hortensio overhears and goes to summon help.

CHECK THE BOOK

Chapter 9 of Martin Wiggins's *Journeymen in Murder: The Assassin in English Renaissance Drama* (Clarendon Press, 1991), called 'Webster's Killers', discusses *The White Devil* and the roles of Flamineo and Lodovico in particular.

Lodovico tells Francisco that he has done enough to avenge his sister, Isabella, and should now leave. He himself will complete the task since he has settled all his personal affairs. Indeed he says he will refuse to continue if Francisco does not depart. Francisco says that he will raise a memorial to him if he should die. Hortensio overhears and decides to summon the guard to put a stop to disorder.

COMMENTARY

This very short scene creates a break in the increasing momentum, explains Francisco's absence in the last scene, and reveals Lodovico as determined on revenge at whatever personal cost. Hortensio's concluding words also indicate that, whatever the outcome of the following events, order will be ultimately restored: 'These strong court factions that do brook no checks / In the career oft break the riders' necks' (lines 14–15) – in other words, those who do not listen to the warnings of others often bring about their own downfall.

GLOSSARY		
6	quite	repay, requite
7	meanest	least important
8	forswear	go back on his sworn oath to do it
10	rear	raise up

SCENE 6

- Flamineo claims a reward from Vittoria for his service to Brachiano and threatens her to kill her for refusing.
- Vittoria and Zanche shoot him and Flamineo makes a dying speech.
- He announces that the guns had no bullets and jumps up again.
- The conspirators enter and kill Zanche, Vittoria and Flamineo.
- Giovanni, Ambassadors and guards arrive.

Flamineo goes to Vittoria and finds her with a book, perhaps a Bible, since he says 'What, are you at your prayers?' (line 1). Their initial exchanges are insulting but it is unclear if this is simply banter. Flamineo demands that Vittoria write down how she will reward him for his service but all she offers is the same 'portion' that 'Cain groaned under having slain his brother' (lines 13–14), that is nothing except to wander the earth. Flamineo is incensed and claims that his lord has left him 'two case of jewels / Shall make me scorn your bounty' (lines 19–20). He returns with two cases of pistols, claiming that he had made a vow to Brachiano that neither of them should outlive the duke by four hours. Vittoria is unsure whether to believe him, questioning his intentions, but Flamineo assures her that he will die with pleasure. She is forced to try to argue herself out of the situation.

Meanwhile Zanche calls for help. Flamineo threatens her and rejects Vittoria's arguments, claiming that they are mere rhetoric, 'grammatical laments, / Feminine arguments' (lines 66–7). Zanche suggests to Vittoria that they humour him and persuade Flamineo to kill himself first. Vittoria at once picks up on her suggestion and changes tack in her argument. Flamineo agrees to their plan but makes them 'first swear / Not to outlive me' (lines 96–7).

Flamineo gives a moving farewell speech about dying, before asking them 'Are you ready?' 'Ready' they reply (line 104). He then launches into a **satirical** vision of purgatory in which the great are reduced to ignominious, inappropriate tasks, before considering his own fate, claiming not to know nor 'greatly care' (line 112) where he will go and ordering the women to shoot. 'Of all deaths the violent death is best' (line 114) he claims **ironically**. They shoot and he falls. They run to him and *tread upon him*. Assuring him of his own 'most assured damnation' (line 120) they refuse to kill themselves. They triumph over him. Vittoria sees his death as adding to her own glory, 'This thy death / Shall make me like a blazing ominous star' (lines 129–30). Flamineo says that he is dying, 'the way's dark and horrid' (line 136), giving graphic details of his sensations.

When they refuse to kill themselves he exclaims, 'O cunning devils!' (line 146), tells them that he has been testing their love and jumps up. This is a dramatic coup de théâtre which is as much a surprise to the audience as to Vittoria and Zanche. It provokes a misogynistic tirade from Flamineo who warns men, 'Trust a woman! Never, never!' (line 158).

At this point the conspirators enter and Vittoria calls 'Help, help!' (line 165) only to be greeted by Lodovico who announces that they 'have brought you a masque' (line 167), that is a courtly entertainment, before calling the name of 'Isabella' and *throw[ing] off their disguises*' (line 169). In an echo of Brachiano's despair in Act I Scene 2 Vittoria exclaims 'O we are lost' (line 172). Flamineo is still furious with Vittoria and angry that he will not now be able to punish her himself, ironically seeing his vengeance as justice. He blames fate, a 'spaniel' (line 175) which dogs us. Lodovico and Gasparo bind him to a pillar.

Vittoria begs for mercy, asking whether Francisco would kill her if he were in the court but Gasparo points out the ironic truth which the play has demonstrated that 'Princes give rewards with their own hands, / But death or punishment by the hands of others' (lines 186–7). Lodovico remembers the occasion when Flamineo struck him and vows to take revenge, but Flamineo objects that he cannot defend himself.

Lodovico continues to taunt Flamineo and Vittoria but they both parry his remarks and show no sign of fear. Vittoria strikes a heroic

CHECK THE BOOK

In Marlowe's play *The Jew of Malta*, there is a similar *coup de théâtre*, that is a 'sensational or dramatic turn of events', when the witty **satirical** hero, Barabas jumps up alive again after being pronounced dead in Act V Scene 1. He is thrown over the city walls, only to rise up when everyone else has left, much to the surprise of the audience.

CONTEXT

The masque developed from the medieval practice of masked revellers arriving at the hall of a nobleman to celebrate a festive occasion to become the sophisticated aristocratic entertainments of the royal court. Masques were often allegorical in nature with a political subtext.

CHECK THE BOOK

Flamineo's claim that Brachiano ordered that Vittoria should not 'outlive him' by 'four hours' (lines 33–4) may have been inspired by Lady Elizabeth Cary's closet drama, *The Tragedy of Mariam, Fair Queen of Jewry* (1613), in which King Herod orders that his wife, Mariam, should be killed when he dies. The play, written between 1602 and 1604 and circulated in manuscript, the first published play to be written by a woman.

CONTEXT

Vittoria's image of her heart as a 'flaming altar' (line 82) appears to be derived from Rollenhagen's continental emblem book (*Nucleus Emblematum*, 1611–13) which shows a flaming heart on an altar as an image of sacrifice to God.

pose reminiscent of Cleopatra in Shakespeare's *Antony and Cleopatra*, insisting on dying before Zanche, 'I will be waited on in death; my servant / Shall never go before me' and claiming that she will welcome death 'As princes do some great ambassadors: / I'll meet thy weapon halfway' (lines 215–9). In the event, the conspirators strike all three simultaneously – 'With a joint motion' (line 229). Vittoria is penitent, acknowledges her fault and that she is duly punished for it, 'O my greatest sin lay in my blood. Now my blood pays for't' (lines 238–9). Flamineo pays tribute to her courage 'Th'art a noble sister—/ I love thee now' (lines 239–40). He recognises her strength and her innate qualities, arguing that 'She hath no faults, who hath the art to hide them' (line 245). Vittoria, however, is dying: 'My soul. Like to a ship in a black storm, / Is driven I know not whither' (lines 246–7). Flamineo encourages her to 'cast anchor' (line 247): death will bring release. For himself, he will not consider the fates of others, 'at myself I will begin and end' (line 256). Vittoria dies regretting the course of her life, 'O happy they that never saw the court, / "Nor ever knew great man but by report"' (lines 259–60).

Flamineo revives briefly and he too ruminates on the way to deal with 'great men' before commenting that 'there's some goodness in my death' and confessing 'My life was a black charnel' (line 268). He has he says 'caught / An everlasting cold. I have lost my voice / Most irrecoverably' (line 269–70). And in a theatrical gesture he bids 'Farewell' to the 'glorious villains' before concluding with a sentimental reflection on life and his wishes for his own funeral arrangements (line 271–4). Flamineo's death is the real climax of the play.

Giovanni, the Ambassadors and guards arrive. The guards shoot the conspirators. Lodovico reveals his identity to Giovanni and that it was his uncle Francisco who ordered the deaths. Giovanni is shocked and orders them all to be taken to prison and tortured. Lodovico is unrepentant, glorying in his revenge – he cares nothing for the punishment that lies in store for him but is vindicated in his own mind by his murderous artistry: '"I limbed [created] this night-piece and it was my best"' (line 295). Giovanni orders the removal of the bodies and offers a moral for the guilty: '"Let guilty men remember their black deeds / Do lean on crutches, made of slender reeds"' (lines 298–9).

COMMENTARY

The final scene is full of surprises, sudden reversals and changes of
tone. The audience may well feel traumatised by the journey on
which they have been taken. The opening section between Flamineo
and Vittoria veers wildly between **tragedy** and comedy. For the
third time in the play Vittoria's rhetorical powers are called upon to
defend herself in a desperate situation. She **ironically** turns to
theological argument to dissuade Flamineo from killing them both:

> Are you grown an atheist? Will you turn your body,
> Which is the goodly palace of the soul,
> To the soul's slaughter house? (lines 54–6)

She blames the devil which presents 'all other sins' as triply
attractive, causing humans to turn away from their rightful goal to
seek hell that belongs to devils instead, arguing he 'Makes us forsake
that which was made for man, / The world, to sink to that was made
for devils, / Eternal darkness' (lines 60–3). In comparison, Flamineo's
jibe that he will have as much pleasure in dying as his father had in
conceiving him is a rare moment of joviality (lines 51–2), aligning
death with the sexual act and eroticising it. This connection between
birth and death is repeated by Flamineo at line 193 when he asks
Lodovico: 'Wouldst have me die, as I was born, in whining?'

We are shocked by what we take to be Flamineo's death at the hands
of Vittoria and Zanche. In a **parody** of a typical death scene in
Renaissance drama, Flamineo describes in graphic detail the
sensations he experiences at the onset of death:

> O I smell soot,
> Most stinking soot, the chimney is a-fire—
> My liver's parboiled like Scotch holy-bread;
> There's a plumber laying pipes in my guts, it scalds; (lines 139–42)

Flamineo's return to life is even more shocking and the tone is
further darkened by the arrival of the conspirators. Vittoria and
Flamineo's courage in the face of death allows them finally to
achieve a sort of tragic stature. Discussing the death of Flamineo,
Alexander Leggatt argues:

 **CHECK
THE POEM**

Critics commonly
point out that in
traditional
theological teaching
the body is
regarded rather as a
'prison'. Renaissance
teaching regarded
the body as less
contemptible than
medieval
scholasticism had
done, and the
image of the soul as
a 'goodly palace'
may be found in
Edmund Spenser's
poem *The Faerie
Queene* (II.20:8).

 **CHECK
THE BOOK**

In *The Duchess of
Malfi*, the duchess
repeats Flamineo's
line 200 'Nothing,
of nothing: leave
thy idle questions'
before her death.

There is no better definition of what we might call the Jacobean world picture: man adrift in an incomprehensible universe, knowing only himself, and even then certain only of his death. (*English Drama: Shakespeare to the Restoration, 1590–1660*, 1988, p. 157)

The final passage in which Giovanni, the Ambassadors and the guards arrive is inevitably an anticlimax. It is fitting that the conspirators are shot but the fate that Giovanni condemns them to is disturbing. His response to Lodovico's revelations of his uncle's involvement leaves the ending unresolved and many questions in the audience's minds.

In place of an Epilogue, Webster uses a maxim from the Latin poet Martial – 'These things will be our reward if I have pleased' (Martial II, xci, 8) – and a brief review of the first performance, praising his 'friend Master Perkins' who played Flamineo.

CONTEXT

Richard Perkins became the leading tragedian with Queen Henrietta's Men from 1625 to the closure of the theatres in 1642 at the outbreak of the English Civil War.

QUESTION

What do you finally think about Flamineo and Vittoria – were they victims of circumstance or were they the agents of their own downfall?

GLOSSARY	
3	**blouze** wench, slattern, 'fat red-faced bloated wench' (used ironically to Zanche)
5	**wormwood** bitter-tasting herb, an emblem of what is bitter and grievous to the soul
16	**agues** fevers, fits of trembling
22	**s.d. two case** each case holds a pair so Flamineo has four guns in total
25	**stones** jewels, precious stones; gun-stones (used for shot)
27	**sparkle** i.e. in an explosion of gunpowder
58	**stibium** black antimony
59	**carouse** drink it down
63	**winter plums** hard dried fruits, i.e. bullets
65	**mandrakes** plants said to shriek when pulled up
66	**grammatical** formal
91	**taster** one who tasted food to test for poison
102	**cupping-glasses** cup-shaped glass vessels in which a vacuum was created by heating, then applied to the skin to draw off blood

GLOSSARY

105–6   **Lucian … purgatory**   Roman philosopher and satirist; his *Menippos* included a journey to the underworld and the ignominious fates of great men

107   **Pompey tagging points**   Roman general defeated by Julius Caesar fixing metal tags on the laces or 'points' which were used to fasten clothing

110   **lists**   strips of cloth used as ties, garters, etc.

111   **resolve**   dissolve

122   **engine**   plot, device

124   **Styx**   In Greek mythology when a god swore an oath, Iris would collect water from this river in Hades and take it back to Olympia to witness it

130   **blazing ominous star**   a comet, regarded as omens of disaster

131   **springe**   snare for catching small game

132   **short home**   empty-handed

132   **braches**   bitches

141   **liver**   regarded as the seat of the passions

      Scotch holy bread   stewed sheep's liver

143-4   **drive … body**   Suicides were traditionally buried at crossroads with a stake driven through the heart to restrain their ghosts

147   **reaches**   schemes, plots

149   **prove**   test

158   **Artillery Yard**   ground in Bishopsgate where citizens and merchants practised the exercise of arms and military discipline

162   **Hypermnestra**   the only one of his fifty daughters who disobeyed her father, Danaus, and did not kill her husband on his wedding night

164   **horse-leeches**   blood-suckers, rapacious people

167   **matachin**   sword dance, related to the morris-dance

181   **pillar**   either one of the pillars supporting the heavens (roof) or a freestanding post on the stage

continued

CHECK THE BOOK

Flamineo's demand for thunder is reminiscent of Vindice, the avenger in *The Revenger's Tragedy* (1606, previously ascribed to Cyril Tourneur but now generally regarded as written by Thomas Middleton) who asks 'Mark, thunder! Dost know thy cue, thou big-voiced crier?' and when he has killed the villains remarks 'No power is angry when the lustful die: / When thunder claps, heaven likes the tragedy'. The noise of thunder was imitated either by drumming or rolling large metal cannon balls backstage. Lightning was produced by fireworks.

CONTEXT

Vittoria blames her fate on her 'blood' (line 238), a word that reverberates throughout **revenge tragedy**, often known as the 'tragedy of blood'. It is a term with multiple meaning in the period: passion, desire/temper, spirit/family. Vittoria's speech seems to play **ambiguously** across all these.

GLOSSARY

194	**Recommend … heaven** i.e. say your prayers
213	**train** tail of a comet, punning on 'attendants' (Zanche)
227	**falling sickness** epilepsy, playing on 'falling' i.e. dying
233	**Toledo … fox** kinds of swords
234	**cutler** one who deals in knives and cutting implements
268	**charnel** charnel house, where the bones of the dead were kept

EXTENDED COMMENTARIES

TEXT 1 – I.2.306–52 (PAGES 24–5)

From 'Now, you that stand' to 'winding and indirect'

Immediately prior to this passage, Brachiano, Duke of Orsino, has just had his first romantic encounter with Vittoria Corombona, engineered and witnessed by her brother, Flamineo. However, their mother, Cornelia, was also watching, and horrified by their adulterous liaison she cursed the duke and her daughter. Vittoria ran from the room and at this point the angry duke has just left the house, making threats as he leaves.

At the opening of the passage, Flamineo blames his mother for her attitude, referring sarcastically to her sense of 'honour' (line 306) and asks her if she thinks it appropriate to send such an aristocrat home alone at night, suggesting that in his mind, at least, 'honour' is related to power and social position. He does not for a moment reflect that it might be the duke and his lack of morality who is to blame for the situation. He then launches into a more general attack on his mother, sarcastically demanding to know the whereabouts of the money she should, in his view, have saved for him to live like a gentleman, and that would prevent him having to serve someone like Brachiano.

Cornelia defends herself and asks the key moral question: does poverty necessarily make a person corrupt? This question is still asked today in discussions of the relationship between poverty and crime. The answer any individual gives will depend on their personal beliefs. Cornelia is voicing the conventional Christian view that being poor should not be an excuse for corrupt or immoral behaviour. Flamineo, however, does not answer directly but continues with his complaint, asking her again what 'means' – **ironically** signifying both 'financial assets' and 'strategies' – she has to keep him from the 'galleys' (sea-going ships manned by oarsmen who were either slaves or condemned criminals) or the 'gallows' (hanging) (lines 13–14). Both these suggest literally that Flamineo regards the inevitable outcome of poverty as crime and death.

Flamineo goes on to detail his family history and fortunes, recounting ironically how his father 'proved himself a gentleman' (line 315) by acting in the way that many of the less prosperous landed gentry were doing at this time. Finding their inherited lands provided insufficient income for their high-spending lifestyles, these nobles sold them and profligately spent the capital. This was considered an evil sign of the times by conservative contemporary commentators, a sign that the old established social patterns of feudalism, where money and position were linked to land ownership, were in decline. The selling of land by traditional aristocrats, often to wealthy self-made men and merchants, signalled social mobility and the increasing power of money and trade. Flamineo's father was lucky, he says, since he died before all the money was spent. Although Flamineo has had the benefit of a university education from Padua, the most ancient and respected university in Italy, he complains that he had not got sufficient money to live on and that he had had to mend his tutor's hose to pay his way.

The exact meaning of his words 'Conspiring with a beard / Made me a graduate,' (lines 321–2) are difficult to determine. He may be saying that he graduated simply by coming of age and reaching physical maturity with the growth of a beard (rather than by achieving any intellectual distinction) but the meaning may be more

---

CONTEXT

Social mobility was still limited but slowly increasing at this time. The problem of how to make his way in the world for a young man without a fortune is the subject of numerous contemporary plays. For every successful and upwardly mobile individual (such as John Webster's father) there were those such as Flamineo who lost out.

 CHECK THE BOOK

De Flores in Middleton and Rowley's play *The Changeling* is another such character who complains, 'though my hard fate has thrust me out to servitude, / I tumbled into the world a gentleman'. He, like Flamineo and Bosola in Webster's *Duchess of Malfi,* undertakes a murderous course to secure his own preferment.

TEXT 1 – I.2.306–52 (PAGES 24–5) continued

CHECK THE BOOK

In *Elizabethan Fictions: Espionage, Counter-espionage and the Duplicity of Fiction in Early Elizabethan Prose Narratives* (Clarendon Press, 1997), R. W. Maslen argues that writing fiction automatically marked men out as potential spies and endowed them with a set of dubious qualifications.

CHECK THE POEM

The idea of the court as exercising a fatally corrupting influence was common in the period. In George Gascoigne's autobiographical poem, *The Green Knight's Farewell to Fancy* (1573), he talks about the 'gloss of gorgeous courts' and of lying 'along in ladies' laps … To fawn and flatter both, I liked sometimes well, / But since I see how vain it is, "Fancy," quoth he, "farewell"' (*The Green Knight: Selected Poetry and Prose,* edited by Roger Pooley, Carcanet Press, 1987).

sinister and suggest that he graduated by entering into some sort of nefarious activity with an older man, possibly of a sexual nature. This may even be an oblique reference to the activities of young men such as Christopher Marlowe who was allowed to graduate from Cambridge despite not completing his studies, because he had been engaged on government business, supposedly spying.

Flamineo reports that he went straight from university into Brachiano's service which perhaps suggests some link between his activities and Brachiano's court. He says that he visited the court and picked up courtly manners and habits in one of many references to the corrupting nature of the court, 'More courteous, more lecherous by far' (line 324) but left without having gained preferment. This again voices a contemporary source of criticism and anxiety: the corruption and corrupt manners of the court. Vittoria refers to it in her final couplet 'O happy they that never saw the court, / "Nor ever knew rich man but by report"' (V.6.259–60). Flamineo sarcastically repeats his question to his mother, asking if since he has such an easy career path before him he should just be a milksop, but answers the question himself in the negative by saying that he will strengthen himself against the shame induced by the corrupt path he has chosen by drinking strong wine.

Cornelia's response to Flamineo's determined course of action is to disown him, wishing that she had never borne him, to which Flamineo's answer is **ironic** agreement. Still referring sarcastically to her sense of propriety, he argues that he would have preferred a common prostitute for a mother since then he would have been well provided for with lots of fathers. He suggests that she should go and complain to the cardinal (Monticelso) but that she may be surprised by his response, since even the renowned Athenian judge and statesman, Lycurgus, had, according to Plutarch, advocated the sharing of wives, not for the benefit of the women but in order to make the most of good breeding-stock. Advising his mother to complain to Monticelso seems ironic in the light of our later knowledge of this corrupt cleric and suggests that Flamineo was only too well aware of his character. Cornelia is dismayed by his answer and she too leaves the room, so that Flamineo is finally alone on stage, sharing his thoughts with the audience in **soliloquy**.

At this point Flamineo reflects on his mother's news, that the duchess (Isabella, Brachiano's wife) has arrived in Rome and that her arrival is likely to upset his plans. We never learn precisely how Cornelia has acquired this piece of information – it might signal that she is in some way connected with Isabella personally, since they are both represented as virtuous and devout, or to Isabella's court generally. Flamineo then reports that he and at least one other are engaged in 'mischief' (line 345) although it is never clear whether his co-conspirators are Vittoria or Brachiano or both. In view of his later curious little tale of the interdependent relationship of the crocodile, the worm and the bird (IV.2.218–31) it may be that he is referring to the plans of all three of them which are designed to benefit each of them in turn. It is typical of Flamineo that he turns to **simile** at the end of this scene to make his argument, suggesting that he is prepared to take unorthodox, crooked ways to achieve his goals. It is also typical that the **imagery** should be naturalistic, including 'rivers' and a 'mountain' and indeed animalistic, a 'snake' (line 348–50). Imagery involving animals almost always represents moral debasement from the human and rational to the baser instincts and desires. The phrase 'the subtle foldings of a winter's snake' is ominous, suggesting a cold serpent-like cunning and corruption and is indeed emblematic of the contrivances of politicians and the main players in Webster's drama.

TEXT 2 – III.2.79–112 (PAGES 57–8)

From 'Whore, what's that?' to 'owes nature nothing'

This passage forms part of the scene of 'The Arraignment of Vittoria' in which she is publicly tried for the murder of Camillo, her husband. At the opening of the scene, Vittoria objected to the Lawyer speaking in Latin and then to the complicated legalistic English jargon he used, so that Cardinal Monticelso, supposedly judge in the case, takes it upon himself to accuse her in person in plain English. Vittoria defends herself and points out the irregularity of such a proceeding. He continues, however, with his accusations. In the absence of any other evidence, Monticelso's main charge against her is of immorality, and just prior to this passage he calls her a whore. Vittoria professes ignorance of the term and demands to know what he means by it.

Monticelso launches into an analysis of the term, painting what he describes as 'their perfect character' (line 80). The analysis of the meaning of 'whore', which Monticelso offers is, as might be expected, negative, hostile and inflammatory. It is couched in bizarre, sometimes contradictory, terms covering a range of ideas from poison to magic; from the cold of a Russian winter to the fires of hell; from taxes to legal documents; they are bells and worse than corpses; they are counterfeit coins. The images Monticelso selects are often strange and unexpected and the tone of his accusation is especially disturbing. It is angry and intensely personal, suggesting an inappropriate emotional investment, the very opposite of any rational examination of the facts. His lurid language suggests both a prurient interest in and erotic fascination with the sexuality the whore represents and at the same time a desperate attempt to deny and expunge it. In the 1996 Royal Shakespeare Company production Philip Voss, playing Monticelso, conducted much of the arraignment whilst leering ostentatiously down at the cleavage of the actor playing Vittoria (Jane Gurnet). One of the elements in his analysis which becomes clear, though, is the dangerous threat which uncontrolled female sexuality represented by the 'whore' was seen to pose to the ordered working of society. Monticelso represents the 'whore' as bringing about chaos in both the natural world and civil society, disrupting the weather, birth and death as well as the normal social business of marriage, taxes, legal inheritance and the economy.

Vittoria coolly rejects any application of Monticelso's character in respect of herself: 'This character scapes me' (line 102). He then accuses her of being full of poison from all creatures and minerals and Vittoria again defies him. The French and English Ambassadors, who have attended her trial and who may be regarded as impartial observers of proceedings, clearly accept Monticelso's account of her moral standing. They say, 'She hath lived ill' (line 107), but add that Monticelso has overstated the case and is too personally engaged: 'the cardinal's too bitter' (line 108). Monticelso then explains his moral argument by characterising vices of increasing severity, as though one led inevitably on to the next. He has explained 'whore' and argues that the 'devil, Adult'ry'

CONTEXT

'Characters' were short studies of social types, inspired by the classical models of Theophrastus. Significantly Webster's friend, Sir Thomas Overbury, was the compiler of a contemporary set of 'characters' and Webster himself is believed to have contributed a number of the studies to his collection.

inevitably follows, and then the 'devil, Murder' enters like the cast of a morality play (lines 109–10). At this point, Francisco interjects to point out that Vittoria's husband has indeed been murdered, making the link in Monticelso's argument explicit.

While the audience question the validity of Monticelso's accusation, Vittoria answers him facetiously, reiterating the Church's teaching that death is to be welcomed as a relief from a wicked life and that Camillo has now fulfilled his debt to nature. Her behaviour throughout the rest of the trial is equally spirited. She defends herself with logic and reasoned argument, whereas her accusers stoop to unsupported accusation and insult. Despite this she is committed to the house of convertites, whereas those we know to be responsible for Camillo's death escape without punishment. The scene as a whole highlights the power of the Church and state and its abuse by corrupt noblemen and clergy. It also recognises the way in which socially powerless women are in fact central to a system based on the legal inheritance of lands, titles and money, through their reproductive function, but by which they are oppressed.

TEXT 3 – IV.2.96–145 (PAGES 86–8)

From 'That hand' to 'Never'

This passage takes place in the house of convertites, the 'house for penitent whores' (line 210) to which Vittoria has been confined after her arraignment by Cardinal Monticelso. Francisco, Isabella's brother, has decided on a subtle form of revenge and sent Vittoria a love-letter in the form of a poem which Brachiano has intercepted. He has fallen for Francisco's trick, believes Vittoria to be unfaithful to him and angrily accuses her of infidelity.

At the opening of this passage, Brachiano takes Vittoria's hand, and curses it and the many times he has foolishly kissed it, and looks back with regret to Isabella, the duchess whom he had had murdered. He echoes Monticelso's accusation against her, complaining that Vittoria has bewitched him, 'For all the world speaks ill of thee' (line 100). Up to now Vittoria has denied his accusations but this rouses her anger and she proudly asserts that

CONTEXT

Morality plays evolved from the medieval mystery play and were popular throughout Europe in the fifteenth and sixteenth centuries. They typically dramatised the passage of the **personified** human soul such as 'Everyman' and a cast of allegorical figures based on abstract characteristics designed to convey and comment on Christian doctrine and precepts.

CHECK THE BOOK

For modern audiences the specifics of usage of 'thou' and 'you' are often lost, or only vaguely understood. Penelope Freedman's *Power and Persuasion in Shakespeare's Pronouns* (Ashgate, 2007) details the most famous early modern playwright's complex, sophisticated usage of these pronouns.

QUESTION

The Romantic critic Charles Lamb found Vittoria's performance in her trial riveting and talks of her 'innocence-resembling boldness' ('A Note on the Arraignment of Vittoria', *Specimens of the English Dramatic Poets Who Lived about the Time of Shakespeare*, 1808. Do you find her performance equally convincing?

her future life will make the world change its opinion of her. She challenges him over the mention of his duchess and when Brachiano says 'Whose death God pardon' she at once confronts him with the truth. Her response is a form of curse 'Whose death God revenge / On thee, most godless Duke' (lines 103–4). At this point, Vittoria noticeably changes her form of address to Brachiano from the polite 'you' to the intimate 'thou', a sign of emotion, both love and scorn, since the term was used to intimates and inferiors. It intensifies the sense of her anger throughout the scene. Her speech also reveals that Vittoria knew that Brachiano was responsible for his wife's death, making it possible that her performance of injured innocence in court was an act. It also reveals Brachiano as weak and hypocritical to disclaim responsibility for Isabella's death and bemoan it in this way. As with so many lightly spoken words in this play, they will return to haunt the speaker. Isabella's death will ultimately be revenged on Brachiano.

Flamineo's **aside** 'Now for two whirlwinds' (line 104) shows that he understands his sister's temperament only too well and that her anger, once roused, is likely to equal the duke's. It suggests that they are well-matched. Both are wild, passionate spirits but also violent and destructive, destroying everything in their path and leaving a trail of ruin in their wake. Vittoria at once launches into an angry rebuttal of Brachiano's accusations, pointing out clearly how much she has lost by her relationship with him – her reputation and position in society. Despite all his promises, he has in fact reduced her to her present degraded position and she suggests that he has ruined other women in the same way. She then, in a magnificent gesture, rejects and dismisses him, 'Fare you well sir; let me hear no more of you' (line 117). Her next remark is a strange mixture of **metaphor**, biblical **allusion** and historical reality:

> I had a limb corrupted to an ulcer,
> But I have cut it off: and now I'll go
> Weeping to heaven on crutches. (lines 118–20)

Is the corrupted limb a **metonym** for Brachiano himself, suggesting that he has become part of her, or does it refer to the corrupt part of herself? The historical duke Bracciano had a malignant ulcer on his leg, which unconsciously connects him with the metaphor. The next part of her speech though echoes the gospel of St Mark 9:45: 'And if thy foot offend thee, cut it off: it is better for thee to enter halt into life, than having two feet to be cast into hell.' This is an excellent example of Webster's complex allusive style, which draws together ideas and phrases from very disparate sources and melds them together to create a dense dramatic world of his own.

Having said that she will return all his gifts, and wishing she could die leaving Brachiano responsible for all her sins, Vittoria says he's not worth shedding 'one tear more' (line 125) for before throwing herself on a bed and weeping. The audience can never be sure with Vittoria what is genuinely felt and what is play-acting. When she speaks she has reason on her side – in her arraignment, she countered Monticelso with logic and was proudly defiant in a way that seemed utterly convincing. We now know that she was aware of Brachiano's responsibility for Isabella's death despite her claims of innocence. Here again she has countered Brachiano's accusations with complete justification – he has reduced her to her present situation and she is certainly justified in telling him so and stating her innocence. But having just said she will not 'shed one tear more' she throws herself down and weeps. Is she weeping from anger, frustration, self-pity or is it simply an act to gain sympathy or some more complex mixture of motives?

Whatever the motive, her action has the desired effect and Brachiano claims to have 'drunk Lethe' (line 126), that is to have forgotten all about it. She has said and done enough to convince him of her honesty with regard to Francisco's letter. Brachiano tries to make it up but Vittoria will now have nothing to do with him and rejects all his advances angrily. When Flamineo attempts to make peace, she turns on him too, calling him 'pander' (line 135), that is a 'pimp' who has prostituted her to Brachiano. When Brachiano declares his undying love of which his jealousy is a symptom, she furiously calls him a 'fool' (line 139) and too big for his boots. She dare suffer anything that he does except continue as his mistress, which nothing can make her do. When he renews his attempts to explain, she continues to reject him angrily, claiming that she will 'Never' (line 145) listen to him. In fact it takes until the end of the scene and the combined efforts of Flamineo and Brachiano to talk

CHECK THE BOOK

The term 'pander' comes from Pandarus, Cressida's uncle in Shakespeare's **satirical** play *Troilus and Cressida*. Shakespeare's main source was Chaucer's narrative poem, *Troilus and Criseyde*, the first English version of the story. He in turn had used Boccaccio's *Il Filostrato*, the first version which suggests his role as a go-between in bringing the lovers together.

her round and that is only once Brachiano has promised to marry her and make her his duchess.

These exchanges offer a brilliant example of the play's sudden reversals of fortune, the way the balance of power within relationships quickly changes. At the beginning of this passage, Vittoria is completely on the defensive and yet by the power of her rhetoric she is able by the end to gain the upper hand over Brachiano and achieve everything that she wants. The tone of the passage is notable – gone are the flowery romantic images of **courtly love** – the language throughout this passage is concerned with disease, crime, corruption and death. The **irony** of all this is that although the participants believe that they are acting of their own free will in fact they are simply falling into the trap that Francisco's superior cunning has set for them.

TEXT 4 – V.6.230–74 (PAGES 149–51)

From 'Twas a manly blow' to 'my farewell'

At the opening of this final dramatic scene, Flamineo has gone to Vittoria to demand recompense for all his services to the duke but she has offered him nothing. He then threatens to kill her and they form a suicide pact with Zanche. The two women attempt to trick Flamineo by pretending to go through with it and shooting him first. Believing they have killed him and are safe, the women rejoice, only to learn that it has all been an elaborate charade and that there were no bullets in the guns. Into the midst of this furious private row burst the conspirators, intent on revenge for Isabella's death on behalf of Francisco. Flamineo has been bound to a pillar and prior to this passage the conspirators have struck Flamineo, Vittoria and Zanche simultaneously 'With a joint motion' (line 230). This passage covers the deaths of all three characters.

Vittoria's response to the blow is angry, jeering defiance, ''Twas a manly blow' (line 230), whereas Flamineo continues his light-hearted commentary, enquiring what sort of blade was used, confiding that he expected to die a violent death and demanding that the conspirators strike more deeply. At the same time as their stance of public defiance, the brother and sister carry on a private, intimate discussion as they both face death. Vittoria looks back and confesses 'my greatest sin lay in my blood' (line 238) but this **ambiguous** term covers a range of meanings from her family lineage (inherited from the profligate father perhaps) to her own passionate spirit or her sexual desires. Now she recognises that she will pay for her sins with her life-blood. Punning ambiguous word-play in conjunction with intelligent analysis seem typical of brother and sister. Even Flamineo is finally moved to pay her affectionate tribute as she goes bravely to her death in words that again seem to echo Macbeth's admiration for Lady Macbeth in Shakespeare's tragedy, 'If woman do breed man / She ought to teach him manhood.' (lines 240–1)

The linking of the soul to a ship at sea was conventional as sinners proverbially died not knowing where they were going. Flamineo endeavours to give his sister courage. His next remark is partly proverbial, part quotation, part religious convention, as he considers 'Prosperity' (line 248) as a character of the sea, bewitching men like a siren, lulling them into a false sense of security so that they fail to see the rocks ahead. He concludes that death puts an end to suffering. He sees that Zanche is dead and that Vittoria is close to death and reflects that it is not true that women have nine lives, before he utters his most memorable lines, which seem to encapsulate his personal philosophy as he claims that he does not look to see who 'went before, nor who shall follow' (line 255). His personal, egocentric claim is 'at myself I will begin and end' (line 256). Such is the claim of all the great over-reachers from the heroes of Marlowe to Milton's Satan in *Paradise Lost*. His next remark seemingly rejects religious authority as he claims that the source of real knowledge is not to be found in heaven, again a statement seen as symbolic of the arrogance of the new secularism and individualism associated with the Renaissance.

CHECK THE BOOK

In Book II of *Paradise Lost* Mammon counsels the rebel angels in hell that they should not seek to confront God's forces, which they can never overcome, but 'seek / Our own good from ourselves, and from our own / Live to ourselves'.

Vittoria dies uttering the conventional thoughts that seek to shift blame on to the glamour and allure of the court and seductive power of great men. When Flamineo says 'I recover like a spent taper' (line 261) the audience wonder momentarily whether he is going to escape again, as we saw him do previously when we thought he was dying, but soon realise that this time he is not play-acting – or is he? Even in death his mind thinks in images, he is 'like a taper' and he is still obsessed by animal imagery and the idea of the power of great men, remembering the lions in the Tower of London and suggesting that it was better for the successful courtier

CHECK THE BOOK

In her classic tale of **gothic** horror, *Frankenstein* (1818), Mary Shelley describes how he creates the Monster by dismembering corpses and then sewing the parts together: 'I collected bones from charnel-houses; and disturbed, with profane fingers, the tremendous secrets of the human frame'.

to remain humble and anticipate gloomy weather even when the sun shone. Interestingly Brachiano had called himself a 'lion' in his discussion with Francisco and Monticelso (II.1.83). Flamineo's next lines are conventionally Christian as he admits the evil of his life which was 'a black charnel' but then he goes on to make a **metatheatrical** joke complaining that he has caught an 'everlasting cold' (line 268–9) and lost his voice. It is, of course, very likely that an actor with such a large part as Flamineo would be rather hoarse by the end of the play and in danger of losing his voice. 'Farewell, glorious villains' (line 270) is addressed to Lodovico and Gasparo but also to the actors playing the roles.

Flamineo's final lines are two pairs of rhyming **couplets**, which fittingly bring a sense of closure. The first pair's proverbial meaning looks something like: 'It is foolish to be busy since doing nothing brings contentment in a world where effort and striving only bring pain' but as so often the opposite interpretation is also possible: 'Effort and striving are in the end useless but doing nothing brings death in a world where all are striving so desperately to succeed'. The last couplet seems addressed to God or those in charge of his funeral arrangements or the stage manager. Rather than bells tolling his funeral knell, he wants 'thunder' to 'strike' (line 274), a powerful omen of the fall of great men and reminiscent of Hieronimo's joke in *The Revenger's Tragedy,* but it may also refer to the offstage pounding on the doors by the Guards and Ambassadors.

After all the busy action across the stage in the previous scenes, this entire passage is a quiet central moment during which the two main characters die. The audience are likely to have powerful but complex feelings towards this pair whose careers we have followed throughout. They have been full of surprises, often behaved badly and yet have won our grudging admiration through their sheer bravery and vitality. Their words are a typical Websterian mix of discourses – proverbial, **allusive** and Christian – which gives the text its density, interspersed with sudden striking lines and images which pierce this texture. Flamineo's, final irreverent **metatheatrical** comments, put him momentarily outside the action of the play, and sum up this complex dramatic stage character.

PART THREE

CRITICAL APPROACHES

STRUCTURE

As will be clear by now the structure of *The White Devil* is complicated and often seems confusing, with many surprising twists and turns. One respected critic, an earlier editor of the play, argues:

> For a start we may say that the plot or structure of *The White Devil* is loose and rambling, a gothic aggregation rather than a steady exposition and development towards a single consummation (J. R. Brown quoted in *John Webster: A Critical Anthology*, ed. by G. K and S. K. Hunter, Penguin Books, 1969, p. 241).

A few years later Ralph Berry summed up the play's structure as 'essentially a pattern of evil-doers and of retribution' (*The Art of John Webster*, Clarendon Press, 1972, p. 78). This is a useful way of thinking about it, but there is no simple distinction in moral terms between the two groups since those carrying out the retribution are at least as evil as the original wrong-doers and dramatically much less attractive.

The event which precipitates the action of the play is the onset of the love affair between Vittoria and Brachiano. This leads to the murder of their spouses, Camillo and Isabella, which leads to the revenge of Monticelso and Francisco. Our sense of the play as we read it is much less straightforward, though, mainly due to the dominant presence of the parallel characters of the two ruined nobles Flamineo and Lodovico, young men employed by Brachiano and Francisco respectively, who are desperate to recover their fortunes and social position at whatever cost.

The play is written in five acts and works with recurrent patterns of public and private scenes, linguistic images, sensational events and dynamic sets of characters, which Webster plays off against each other. The action alternates between Flamineo, Vittoria and

 QUESTION

What is particularly **'gothic'** about the structure of *The White Devil?*

CONTEXT

The five-act structure of Renaissance plays was derived from the practice of Seneca and comic Roman writers such as Terence and Plautus. This structure was less important in the outdoor public theatres with their fast-paced fluid acting style but private indoor theatres needed regular breaks in performance for the candles to be replaced which lit the auditorium.

Brachiano on the one hand and the opposing group, consisting of Francisco, Monticelso, Lodovico, on the other. Each set of characters follow narrative trajectories of their own, coming together in scenes of dramatic confrontation.

The action can be divided in a number of ways. The first four acts chart the trials, tribulations and ultimate success of the relationship between Brachiano and Vittoria: the love affair plot. In the manner of a *de casibus* tragedy, the play charts the rise and fall of a great man precipitated by the operation of the wheel of Fortune. At the beginning of Act V the celebration of his marriage to Vittoria represents the zenith of his fortunes. Once this is achieved, however, the alternate motion is immediately put into play, the wheel turns and all is lost. However, the play never seems to allow such a simple analysis. The actions undertaken by Brachiano, Flamineo and Vittoria in order to achieve their desires have led to the setting in motion of the revenge plot by the other characters. This ensures that the stability they achieve will not last. Brachiano's apparent success runs parallel to the elevation of Cardinal Monticelso to Pope, Lodovico's pardon and Francisco's determination to seek private revenge for his sister's death.

Webster alternates scenes between the public and the private suggesting parallel characters and events: for example, Act I Scene 1, in which Gasparo and Antonelli reprimand Lodovico for his behaviour, parallels Act II Scene 1, in which Monticelso and Francisco reprimand Brachiano. Webster exploits the dramatic effect of a spectacular public scene rapidly giving way to an intense private confrontation, for example also in Act I Scene 2, in which Brachiano makes a grand entrance with his attendants only to dismiss them, is paralleled by his entrance in Act II Scene 1, in which he no sooner enters than Francisco gives the order to 'Void the chamber' (II.1.19). Vittoria has to defend herself twice, in public in Act III Scene 2 and in private in Act IV Scene 2. There are two **dumb shows**, two ghosts, two processions, two **malcontents** (Flamineo and Lodovico), two dukes, two duchesses; Isabella dies of poison after kissing Brachiano's portrait; Brachiano dies of poison after his lips touch the beaver of his helmet. This pattern of repetition with variation is built up throughout the play, which gives it a characteristically dense, rich texture.

CHARACTERISATION

FLAMINEO

Flamineo is clearly the main character in terms of the length and intellectual energy of his part. His role is central and his death marks the climax of the play but he is nevertheless not the most important character in plot terms. It can be argued to what extent the play is 'about' him at all. His story is relatively unimportant in the events of the play. He is the Duke of Brachiano's secretary and Vittoria's brother – and he lives and dies through them. But he functions as the main conduit of information for the audience with whom in his numerous **asides** and **soliloquies** he builds up a relationship. It is not a very comfortable relationship though; as we come to know him better we learn to distrust him and to disapprove of his character and actions, while at the same time being entertained by his outrageous insolence and hoping that somehow he might be redeemed. He is attractive and repellent at the same time; the play comes alive when he is on stage, but this attraction forces the audience to consider their own moral position when they find themselves colluding with such an amoral character.

Modern psychology would perhaps diagnose his personality type as 'psychopathic' given his glibness and superficial charm, lack of emotional empathy, manipulative behaviour, parasitic lifestyle and so on, but a contemporary early modern way of understanding his character would have been in terms of the four humours: sanguine, phlegmatic, choleric and melancholic. Flamineo's general behaviour indicates a surfeit of 'black bile' leading to 'melancholy'. Such a character was a popular figure in early modern drama; notable examples include Malevole (in Marston's *The Malcontent*), Mercutio (in Shakespeare's *Romeo and Juliet*), Jaques (in Shakespeare's *As You Like It*), Iago (in Shakespeare's *Othello*), Bosola (in Webster's *The Duchess of Malfi*), Richard III and Hamlet. Characters can then be sometimes less, sometimes more, sympathetic. Flamineo is a typical malcontent: he is unhappy and dissatisfied with the world and his own lot in life, and from his position as a relative outsider, he offers a cynical commentary on events and characters in the play.

> **CONTEXT**
>
> Flamineo was historically the name of Vittoria's innocent younger brother but Webster swapped the names round, understandably, for the resonance of fire and flames in Flamineo.

> **CONTEXT**
>
> The theory of the four humours in medieval and Renaissance physiology was derived from Greek and Roman physicians, notably Hippocrates and later Galen, who thought of the body as composed of four substances: blood, phlegm, black bile, yellow bile. These were in balance in a healthy individual. An imbalance of the humours led to various morbid conditions which had an effect on a character's health and temperament.

CONTEXT

Flamineo was also one of the names of the typical young lover in the Italian *Commedia dell'arte* (comedy of art or of the profession) a tradition of improvisational masked comedy which emerged in Tuscany in the middle of the fourteenth century and continued as a popular art form for four hundred years.

His own analysis of the problem with his life, and what has made him the person he is, is want of money, the lack of financial support from his family which he feels he was entitled to. In Act I Scene 2, he blames his mother for his situation:

> I would fain know where lies the mass of wealth
> Which you have hoarded for my maintenance,
> That I may bear my beard out of the level
> Of my lord's stirrup? (I.2.309–12)

In order to advance himself in the world he has therefore become Brachiano's secretary and is, as he puts it, 'prompt / As lightening' (I.2.4–5) to his service. He is in fact willing to prostitute his sister and murder his brother-in-law in order to serve this corrupt duke and advance his own interests. Nevertheless we know that in reality he dislikes and despises Brachiano, as he makes clear on the one occasion where he confronts him in the house of convertites. He understands the duke's character perfectly as he tells him, 'As in this world there are degrees of evils: / So in this world there are degrees of devils' (IV.2.56–7).

Given his many gifts: his wit, intelligence and power to amuse, the course of action which he has chosen is tragic, giving the audience a sense of what he might have become if he had only chosen to follow a different course in life. On the other hand, no one has more of a sense of his own potential greatness than himself and this arrogance marks him out for disaster as he constantly treats others with cynical contempt. His **asides** about Camillo (Act I Scene 2) are amusing, but the cold-hearted murder which follows is not. The overhearing of his remarks about Giovanni is unfortunate but deserved and the insolent remarks addressed to the child as he points out the advantages of his father's death are callous, 'You're now, my lord, i'th'saddle' (V.4.19).

Flamineo constantly harps on about himself, his own ill-treatment and lack of appreciation. Such egocentricity is well captured in his dying remark, 'at myself I will begin and end' (V.6.256). He never really seems to think or care about anyone else. Only towards the end of the play, when everything is unravelling, do we see any glimpse of feeling for others. This is evident when he sees his distracted mother and comments:

I have a strange thing in me, to th'which
I cannot give a name, without it be
Compassion. (V.4.110–112)

It is also apparent in the admiration he expresses for Vittoria as she
faces death unflinchingly: 'Th'art a noble sister – / I love thee now'
(V.6.239–40). A disturbing element in his commentary is his
misogyny, that is his constant complaints against and belittling of
women, which, it is true to say, resonates with the sentiments of
many of the play's other characters.

VITTORIA

Vittoria is a more enigmatic character than her brother. The
audience are given no opportunity to build up an intimate rapport
with her and learn the secrets of her heart. As the critic and editor
John Russell Brown points out in each of the scenes in which she
appears, 'her mood, or tone, is very different' and he goes on to add
that 'For an actress this presents a great difficulty, for there is no
build-up of presentation; each of Vittoria's scenes starts on a new
note, with little or no preparation in earlier scenes' (Introduction to
Brown's 1960 edition, p. xlviii, reprinted in *John Webster: A Critical
Anthology*, p. 245). It presents difficulties also in analysing her as a
character. Nevertheless her role is central in a way that her brother's
is not and she is the focus of the love plot. Her beauty is dwelt on at
length. She is 'the fair Vittoria' (I.2.6) and 'Excellent devil' (1.2.254)
wearing white at the beginning of Act V in the wedding procession;
she likens herself to a 'diamond' (III.2.294). She is also, therefore,
one of, if not the, main candidate for the title role of 'White Devil'.

Despite her centrality to the plot, Vittoria has only six appearances:
Act I Scene 2 when she sees Brachiano alone for the first time; we
then do not see her until Act III Scene 2 in her arraignment; after
being condemned as a whore, we next see her in the house of
convertites in Act IV Scene 2; she is not seen then until the wedding
procession at the beginning of Act V, at Brachiano's death in Act V
Scene 3 and lastly at her own death in the final scene, Act V Scene 6.
Given the very different nature of these scenes, it is difficult to form
a judgement about her character since we mainly see her in
conjunction with other characters, especially male characters, and
forced to respond to situations which they have created.

QUESTION

Do you consider
Flamineo or
Vittoria the main
character in the
play? Does it make
a difference to
your
understanding
whether you
regard brother or
sister as the central
character?

QUESTION

Is Vittoria more sinned against than sinning in being married off to a man she does not love, or is she a scheming ambitious adventuress on the make? What evidence can you find for or against her?

What we see of Vittoria is her coolness when confronted by Monticelso's accusations in court and her proud, spirited defence in the face of the abuse of his position and legal powers. As she says:

> Sum up my faults I pray, and you shall find
> That beauty and gay clothes, a merry heart,
> And a good stomach to feast, are all,
> All the poor crimes that you can charge me with: (III.2.207–10)

The audience must ask themselves whether this is an accurate portrait – is she in fact just a good-time girl or is she an ambitious, hypocritical schemer, a 'White Devil' willing to stop at nothing, including inciting murder, to gain her ends?

When condemned as a whore Vittoria defies the court and proudly proclaims, 'It shall not be a house of convertites. / My mind shall make it honester to me / Than the Pope's palace' (III.2.289–92). Her final words as she exits the court ring with all the power of injured innocence: 'Know this, and let it somewhat raise your spite, / Through darkness diamonds spread their richest light' (III.2.293–4). Vittoria's performance throughout this scene is utterly convincing, in what the Romantic critic Charles Lamb referred to admiringly as her 'innocence-resembling boldness', but for the nagging doubt at the back of the audience's mind that she was in some way responsible for the deaths of her husband and Isabella.

In the house of convertites she is again in the position of defending herself, this time to Brachiano against his accusation that she is unfaithful to him. This time we are sure of her innocence but, in defending herself, she lets slip that she knows about Brachiano's guilt in his wife's death, so that we are bound to question her moral position. If we are never sure of her feelings for Brachiano, neither are we sure what she feels for Flamineo. Are brother and sister in league, trying to make their way in the world together or are they cynically using each other? Flamineo is not sure either and tests her in the last act where she shows quite clearly that she is happy to shoot him. The audience must ask themselves to what extent her actions are justified – was she simply acting in self-defence since he had threatened to kill her and he had also killed their brother? However when confronted by the conspirators who break in and wound her together with Zanche and Flamineo, Vittoria shows the

same courage and spirit as in her trial in facing death. She and
Flamineo seem to be finally reconciled and her words suggest
remorse for her deeds as she talks of her 'sin' (V.6.238) and her
'soul' (V.6.246). Her final words recognise her errors but
nevertheless she attempts to exonerate herself, 'O happy they that
never saw the court, / "Nor ever knew great man but by report"'
(V.6.259–60).

BRACHIANO

The Duke of Brachiano, one of the most powerful and important
men in Renaissance Italy, is a central character. It is his passion for
Vittoria Corombona which sparks off the events of the play. He is a
mixture of weakness, brutality and bullying. At first he seems weak,
a would-be lover, dependent upon his clever secretary, Flamineo, to
help him achieve his desires. Later he is revealed as vicious, sadistic
and unscrupulous. He appears to be a comic figure as Flamineo
urges him to hide in a cupboard while he persuades Camillo to leave
Vittoria alone for the night so that she can meet the duke. At their
first meeting Vittoria is very much in control in the relationship and
it is she who, by recounting her 'dream', suggests the murder of her
husband and Brachiano's wife. When Cornelia, Vittoria's mother,
accuses them of adultery, he is quick to blame Cornelia for making a
fuss rather than himself for his illegitimate desires:

> Uncharitable woman, thy rash tongue
> Hath raised a fearful and prodigious storm.
> Be thou the cause of all ensuing harm. (I.2.303–5)

When, however, he is confronted by his brother-in-law, Francisco
de Medici, Duke of Florence, over the affair he is unrepentant and
threatens to go to war rather than give Vittoria up. He allows
himself to be calmed by Monticelso but his arrogance and self-
importance are evident in the tone he takes and the way he
characterises himself. He asks Francisco, 'Have you proclaimed a
triumph that you bait / A lion thus?' (II.1.82–3).

Brachiano is an affectionate father, proud of his precocious son,
Giovanni, but a cruel husband, treating Isabella with callous
contempt. Rejecting her attempts at reconciliation he divorces her
but then goes through the charade of letting Isabella divorce him in

> **CONTEXT**
>
> Bracciano is a small
> town in the Italian
> region of Lazio,
> thirty kilometres
> north-west of
> Rome and famous
> for its volcanic
> lake. It flourished
> under the rule of
> the Orsini in the
> sixteenth century
> and became a
> centre for culture.
> Paolo Giordano
> Orsini was made
> Duke of Bracciano
> on his marriage to
> Isabella de Medici,
> daughter of the
> Grand Duke of
> Tuscany.

public in order to avoid war between Florence and Padua, the city states of the two dukes. A mere ten lines after her exit, Brachiano is planning Isabella's murder (II.1.289). The method, by poisoning the portrait of her husband that she kisses each night, underlines his calculating viciousness, as does the gleeful voyeurism of the **dumb show** which he witnesses. His appearance at Vittoria's arraignment is a sign of arrogance, but he threatens violence and departs when Monticelso accuses him in public of lust, leaving Vittoria to defend herself. In the house of convertites he is quick to believe that Vittoria is unfaithful to him, but faced with her anger he backs down.

The character who understands him best is his secretary Flamineo and after his death, he offers this damning assessment of Brachiano's character to the disguised Francisco:

> He was a kind of statesman that would sooner have reckoned how many cannon bullets he had discharged against a town, to count his expense that way, than how many of his valiant and deserving subjects he lost before it. (V.3.62–6)

As Flamineo perceives, he is selfish and immoral, putting his personal desires before everything. On the other hand he does it all for love of Vittoria and when he realises that he is dying his first thoughts are of her, 'Where's this good woman? Had I infinite worlds / they were too little for thee. Must I leave thee?' (V.3.18–19).

FRANCISCO

Francisco de Medici is Duke of Florence and brother of Isabella. He is the perfect embodiment of the Renaissance prince, and a rare 'Machiavellian' (V.3.195) as Flamineo puts it: a clever, sophisticated, ruthless and subtle character type as described by Niccolò Machiavelli in his book *The Prince*, written to gain the favour of an earlier Medici. When we first see him in Act II Scene 1, he expresses concern for Isabella, who has come to Rome having learned of her husband's affair with Vittoria, and takes her part, angrily accusing Brachiano. When Isabella, however, utters her public tirade against her husband and divorces him, Francisco instantly turns against her, 'Now by my birth you are a foolish, mad, / And jealous woman' (II.1.263–4) and blames her for failing to achieve a reconciliation with her husband.

He plots with Monticelso to keep Vittoria's husband out of the way in order for Brachiano's affair with Vittoria to become a public scandal, and is party to her arraignment for her husband's death. It is Francisco who dismisses the verbose lawyer and who points out the improbability of her husband's death being an accident, while publicly acknowledging that there is insufficient evidence for a conviction despite the suspicious circumstances. On learning of his sister's death he appears genuinely moved, 'Believe me I am nothing but her grave' (III.2.340). When Monticelso suggests revenge upon Brachiano, though, Francisco rejects the idea, asking 'Shall I defy him, and impose a war / Most burdensome on my poor subjects' necks, / Which at my will I have not power to end?' (IV.1.5–7). This suggests a difference between himself and Brachiano, whose instant recourse was to violence and the threat of war and, as Flamineo pointed out, without regard to his subjects' sufferings. Francisco is clearly a subtle operator. He even rejects Monticelso's suggestion of 'undermining' (IV.1.13) Brachiano publicly, although he keeps Monticelso's 'black book' (IV.1.33) filled with the names of murderers and other malefactors.

In fact Francisco has already decided to take his revenge in his own way, but he does not make Monticelso his ally and in a short **soliloquy** shows his good opinion of himself and his contempt for the cardinal: 'Your flax soon kindles, soon is out again, / But gold slow heats, and long will hot remain' (IV.1.37–40). Francisco's revenge is inspired by Isabella's ghost. The love-letter he sends to Vittoria has the desired effect of making Brachiano jealous and determined to marry her. Francisco then disguises himself as the Moor, Mulinassar, and is accepted as such by Brachiano's court, suggesting fine acting abilities since even Marcello fails to recognise him. Meanwhile he has hired Lodovico, Gasparo, and others to implement Brachiano and Vittoria's deaths. He departs before the end. As Gasparo points out to Vittoria, 'Princes give rewards with their own hands, / But death or punishment by the hands of others' (V.6.186–7). Francisco's absence, at the end of the play, when the villains are caught and punished is disquieting. His survival suggests that his power puts him beyond the reach of the law and that his influence will live on, perhaps in his nephew, the young prince Giovanni.

 CHECK THE BOOK

The term 'Machiavellian' had become synonymous with ruthless cunning. Christopher Marlowe, for example, in the prologue to his play *The Jew of Malta*, (1589–92) describes his protagonist, Barabas, as 'a rich and famous Jew / Who lived in Malta: you shall find him still, / In all his projects, a sound Machevill, / And that's his character'.

MONTICELSO

Cardinal Monticelso is Camillo's uncle. He is Brachiano's enemy and determined to punish him and Vittoria for their affair. He is happy to play with Camillo's life when he sends him off to capture pirates in order to get him out of Brachiano's way:

> It may be objected I am dishonourable
> To play thus with my kinsman, but I answer,
> For my revenge I'd stake a brother's life
> That being wronged durst not avenge himself. (II.1.390–3)

Since the Bible explicitly prohibits acts of private revenge, Monticelso condemns himself out of his own mouth and reveals himself as a corrupt, scheming cleric. When Camillo dies in suspicious circumstances it is Monticelso who presides over Vittoria's arraignment, accusing her of immorality and, in the absence of evidence of her involvement in Camillo's death, sentences her to detention in the house of convertites. Throughout her trial it is Monticelso who plays the leading role, abusing his clerical position, as Vittoria points out, by acting both as her accuser and her judge. Nevertheless his position allows him to act with impunity. His angry tone throughout the proceedings casts him in an unfavourable light. The Ambassadors comment that he is 'too bitter' (III.2.108) and his denunciation of Vittoria appears almost unhinged at times. He seems obsessed by her and her sexual attractions.

CHECK THE BOOK

Shakespeare's play *Measure for Measure* is centrally concerned with hypocrisy and the abuse of authority. The main characters are a novice nun called Isabella and a duke disguised as a friar called Lodovick.

Monticelso is, in fact, the other main candidate for the title role of the 'White Devil' since as Pope he would be clothed all in white despite the fact that his acts by no means match his religious office. Criticism of the clergy, especially the Catholic clergy, was conventional in early modern drama in England after the Reformation, and portraits of corrupt, scheming clerics abound (for example in Shakespeare's *King John*). Monticelso's elevation to Pope, without a proper election, suggests the corruption of the whole institution of the Catholic Church and the fact that his first act on taking up his office, specifically after preaching the 'forgiveness of sins' is to carry out a private act of vengeance by excommunicating Brachiano and Vittoria, reveals its depth. Possession of his 'black book' of Italian malefactors and his urging of Francisco to take revenge reveals a depraved mind. Monticelso, though, is an opaque character in many ways. What is the audience to make of his response when Lodovico confesses his intention to murder Brachiano? Monticelso tells him it is 'damnable' (IV.3.118) and memorably asks 'Dost thou imagine thou canst slide on blood / And not be tainted with a shameful fall?' (IV.3.119–120). Whether or not he is sincere, the effect of Monticelso's advice would have persuaded Lodovico to refrain, had not Francisco sent him money pretending it was from Monticelso. Was Monticelso sincere, then, in his change of heart? Had the holiness of his office finally made him understand the significance of his actions or was he simply paying lip-service to morality? Is he a hypocrite, a 'white devil' or does he embody a religious **paradox**: a corrupt human vessel who can nevertheless deliver God's message, despite his lapsed state?

LODOVICO

Lodovico is a parallel character to Flamineo in many ways, a ruined nobleman, a **malcontent**, and Francisco's murderous henchman, as Flamineo is Brachiano's. Like Flamineo his own story is peripheral to the plot and yet his actions are central. Lodovico has been called 'an artist in murder' (Alexander Leggatt, *English Drama: Shakespeare to the Restoration, 1590–1660*, Longman, 1988, p. 155) and the play opens and closes with him (apart from Giovanni's final **quatrain**). His character is revealed from the start as his two friends, Gasparo and Antonelli, attempt to reconcile him to his banishment, pointing out that his punishment is well deserved. He has lived riotously and ruined himself and committed 'certain murders here in Rome, / Bloody and full of horror' (I.1.31–2). These Lodovico dismisses as 'flea-bitings' (I.2.32). He seems to have no redeeming qualities, but he shares Flamineo's ability to analyse character, **ironically** passing judgement on Flamineo himself as one of 'These rogues that are most weary of their lives' (III.3.128). His motivation in avenging Isabella's death is complicated by his personal feelings for her. He confesses to Monticelso, 'Sir, I did love Brachiano's Duchess dearly; / Or rather I pursued her with hot lust, / Though she ne'er knew on't' (IV.3.112–14).

When Monticelso tells him revenge is 'damnable' (IV.3.118) Lodovico appears willing to 'give it o'er' (IV.3.129) and only reconsiders when he receives money to continue which he believes

 CHECK THE NET

Lodovico awards himself the artistic credit for the carnage of the final act, claiming that he 'limbed this night-piece' (line 295), that is painted (limned) this tragedy (night-piece), perhaps playing on the sense of 'dismember'. Night-pieces were much admired but usually featured religious themes such as Hugo van der Goes's *The Nativity at Night* (1520–30). Go to **www.national gallery.org** and put 'night pieces' into the search box to see a selection.

to be from Monticelso. It is true that he serves Francisco loyally, even insisting he leave Padua before the end: 'My lord, leave the city/ Or I'll forswear the murder' (V.5.1–7). In the event he takes violent bloody revenge and is utterly unrepentant, facing his punishment and torture with equanimity, relishing the artistic effect of his work: 'I do glory yet / That I can call this act mine own: for my part, / The rack, the gallows, and the torturing wheel / Shall be but sound sleeps to me' (V.6.291–5).

ISABELLA

Isabella is Brachiano's wife, Francisco's sister and Giovanni's mother. She is virtuous and devoted to her husband even after he has divorced her. Her murder is effected by poisoning the portrait of Brachiano which she kisses each night. She has been a devoted mother, nursing her son herself at a time when aristocratic women rarely did so, and she is willing to pretend to divorce her husband in public in order to prevent a war between the republics of Florence and Padua. She believes in the power of her love to reconcile her husband claiming that 'these arms / Shall charm his poison … And keep him chaste from an infected straying' (II.1.14–18).

But when Brachiano rejects her and she enacts her public divorce, Isabella's performance convinces her brother. She regrets her female weakness – 'O that I were a man, or that I had power / To execute my apprehended wishes' – but her fierce words 'I would whip some with scorpions' (II.1.242–4) make the audience suspect that Isabella harbours these bitter feelings in her heart, despite her claim that it is purely an act. Her parting words are spoken as an **aside** 'Those are the killing griefs which dare not speak' (II.1.276–7).

ZANCHE

Zanche is Vittoria's maid and Flamineo's mistress. She is very like the brother and sister in being quick-witted, lively, and changeable as she attempts to make her way in an uncompromising world. She is a Moor, originally meaning 'a native or inhabitant of ancient Mauretania, a region of North Africa corresponding to parts of present-day Morocco and Algeria'; later used more loosely to signify 'a member of a Muslim people of mixed Berber and Arab descent inhabiting north-western Africa' (*Oxford English Dictionary*) who conquered Spain in the eighth century. At the time,

CHECK THE BOOK

There is a new biography of Isabella de Medici by Caroline P. Murphy, *Isabella de Medici: The Glorious Life and Tragic End of a Renaissance Princess* (Faber and Faber, 2008). It details Isabella's many love affairs but also highlights her role as a patron of the arts and offers a very different perspective from Webster's on these events.

the cultural associations surrounding people of colour were generally negative although Webster plays with contrasting ideas of black and white in this drama, suggesting that they are interchangeable concepts. Sexual promiscuity is assumed of her, for example, and at Vittoria's arraignment, Monticelso believes Zanche to be Vittoria's 'bawd' (III.2.264) (much to Flamineo's relief) and sentences her with her mistress. Zanche is called 'devil' by Marcello 'Why doth this devil haunt you?' (V.1.86) and he tells Flamineo 'She is your shame' (V.1.91). Cornelia likewise calls her a 'haggard' – meaning 'wild hawk'/ 'promiscuous woman' – (V.1.185) and strikes her, telling her to fly to the 'stews' (V.1.185), that is 'brothel'. It may be that Cornelia and Marcello simply object to the sexual relationship with Flamineo but the terms of their objection seem to be on account of her colour. Their treatment of Zanche, striking and kicking her, is clearly inappropriate, nor does Flamineo treat her well, admitting that he promised marriage but does not intend to keep his promise:

> 'Faith, I made to her some such dark promise and in seeking to fly from't I run on, like a frighted dog with a bottle at's tail that would fain bite it off and yet dares not look behind him. (V.1.157–160)

On the other hand when Francisco adopts a Moorish disguise she at once confesses her love for him and is willing to steal from Vittoria and run away with him. When Flamineo suggests a suicide pact with Vittoria, she calls him 'my best self Flamineo' (V.6.86) as she endeavours to persuade him to let them kill him first. When she believes him to be dying, though, she gloats, telling him he is going 'to most assured damnation' (V.6.120) but she is resolute and dies bravely at the end. When Carlo says 'thou art my task, black fury' (V.6.225), she replies defiantly and, in the same way as Flamineo and Vittoria, is able to make a sardonic joke about her colour in death, 'Death cannot alter my complexion, / For I shall ne'er look pale.' (V.6.225–9).

CORNELIA

Cornelia is the mother of Flamineo, Vittoria and Marcello. She represents the voice of conventional Christian morality in her disapproval of the affair between her daughter Vittoria and

CHECK THE BOOK

See Emily Carroll Bartels, 'Too Many Blackamoors: Deportation, Discrimination, and Elizabeth I', in *Studies in English Literature 1500–1900*, 46:2 (2006), pages 305–22, for details of the lives of black immigrants to England in the early modern period.

QUESTION

How do you view Flamineo's relationship with Zanche? Is it based simply on lust, or to help him promote his schemes for Vittoria?

CONTEXT

Cornelia was the name of one of the most famous and virtuous Roman matrons, the daughter of Scipio Africanus, the hero of the second Punic War (against Hannibal), and wife of Tiberius Gracchus. She was known as the mother of the Gracchi (who were Roman social reformers) and regarded as the ideal of womanhood.

QUESTION

To what extent do you think Webster's use of the name 'Cornelia' with its classical associations is **ironic**?

CHECK THE NET

For details of the custom of giving dowries go to: **http://www. elizabethan-era. org.uk** and click on 'Elizabethan Life'.

Brachiano as she hysterically condemns them, calling Brachiano 'adulterous Duke' (I.2.282) and cursing her daughter: 'May'st thou be envied during his short breath, / And pitied like a wretch after his death' (I.2.296–8).

Nevertheless she accepts her daughter's marriage to Brachiano and is part of the wedding celebrations in Act V. It is there that she voices her disapproval of Flamineo's relationship with Zanche and strikes her. Assuming that the cause of her disapproval is again moral, there is nevertheless a world of difference in her attitude to Zanche and to Brachiano. While she fearlessly condemned Brachiano to his face, she strikes Zanche, presumably on account of her gender and her social inferiority, and also perhaps her colour. When Flamineo kills his brother Cornelia is distraught but nevertheless attempts to shield Flamineo from blame, since he is the only son she has left. It is her descent into madness, modelled on Ophelia's madness in *Hamlet*, as she sings a dirge, 'Call for the robin-red-breast and the wren' (V.4.92), which finally causes Flamineo to feel 'Compassion' (V.4.112).

CAMILLO

Camillo is Vittoria's husband and Monticelso's nephew. From the beginning, though, it is apparent that he is a fool and no match for his beautiful, clever wife. From what we learn of Vittoria's position, through Flamineo's complaints to his mother, it becomes apparent that the family has lost all their money so that her motive for marrying Camillo was financial. At her arraignment Monticelso says to Vittoria, 'He bought you of your father' (III.2.238) and complains that Camillo had spent twelve thousand ducats in six months but received no dowry. Camillo's main function is to obstruct the play's more important characters who are all anxious to get him out of the way. Monticelso packs him off so that Brachiano and Vittoria can continue their affair and become a public scandal; Vittoria plays along with Flamineo to get him out of the way of Brachiano. Flamineo calls him 'an ass' (I.2.51). He is fearful of being cuckolded by Brachiano but gullible and easily manipulated by uncle, wife and brother-in-law. His death at Flamineo's hands, by having his neck broken on a vaulting horse, is pathetic and ignominious.

MARCELLO

Marcello is brother to Flamineo and Vittoria. Whilst Flamineo can be said to represent the medieval/Renaissance character type 'melancholic', Marcello, according to his brother is 'choleric' (V.2.200), that is with an excess of yellow bile, signifying easily angered and bad-tempered. He is a soldier and younger than his brother. He serves Francisco, Duke of Florence, and although poorly rewarded for his service, does not share Flamineo's general discontent. Like his mother, Cornelia, he functions through much of the play as the voice of conventional morality. For example, he frowns on the relationship between Vittoria and Brachiano exclaiming:

> O my unfortunate sister!
> I would my dagger's point had cleft her heart
> When she first saw Brachiano. (III.1.30–2)

This may perhaps make the audience wonder whether conventional morality in which family honour was served by a woman's death is really a preferable alternative. Like Cornelia though, Marcello seems to have overcome his misgivings about the relationship sufficiently to attend the wedding. To Francisco (disguised as Mulinassar) he claims, 'I have been a soldier too' (V.1.114) which suggests that he is no longer, especially in conjunction with Flamineo's taunt 'With a fan of feathers?' (V.2.198) when he says he will cut Zanche's throat. It is difficult to account for the strength of his dislike of Zanche unless it is based on her colour and his fear of interracial marriage: 'I had rather she were pitched upon a stake / In some new-seeded garden, to affright / Her fellow crows thence' (V.1.193–6).

Whatever his feelings about this, to threaten to cut her throat and to kick Zanche in public shows an unpleasant side to his nature. He and his brother are due to fight a duel over the matter but Flamineo unexpectedly rushes at Marcello, killing him and it is his death which causes their mother to lose her mind.

GIOVANNI

Giovanni is the son of Brachiano and Isabella. As Muriel Bradbrook has observed, 'For a minor part it is strongly high-lighted' (*John*

CHECK THE BOOK

Interracial sex and marriage or 'miscegenation' was seen as 'unnatural'. The difficulties and animosity such a partnership could provoke is dramatised in Shakespeare's *Othello* (1603).

CHECK THE BOOK

Muriel Bradbrook's book *John Webster Citizen and Dramatist* (1980) provides a fascinating account of Webster's London and his family's rise, as well as some of the most notable characters of the age, such as Penelope Devereux (sister of the Earl of Essex and the 'Stella' of Sidney's *Astrophil and Stella*) and Antonio Lopez, the Jewish doctor hanged (almost certainly on trumped up evidence) for attempting to poison Queen Elizabeth I.

Webster: Citizen and Dramatist, Weidenfeld and Nicolson, 1980, p. 122). His few brief appearances are designed to display his youth and immaturity. We first see him in Act II Scene 1, in which he arrives in Rome with his mother, emphasising his attachment to her. His main function in the scene is to cement the relationship between his father and uncle. As Monticelso points out, 'here comes a champion / shall end the difference between you both' (II.1.95–6) and this is successful to an extent. The lengthy dialogue with his father and uncle demonstrates his lively intelligence and precocity.

The next time we see him is again in Rome, this time with Lodovico when he has come to tell his uncle of his mother's death. His youthful response to her death provokes pity as he innocently asks his uncle what the dead do, 'Do they eat, / Hear music, go a-hunting, and be merry, / As we that live?' (III.2.323–5). When Francisco replies that they sleep Giovanni confesses that he has not been able to sleep for six nights and that his mother could not sleep for weeping. His narration of her treatment, 'They wrapped her in a cruel fold of lead, / And would not let me kiss her' (III.2.332–4) is reminiscent of Ophelia in *Hamlet*, as she recounts the treatment of her father, Polonius, after his murder. His distress upsets Francisco who instantly vows vengeance.

When we see Giovanni again, this revenge has been started with his father's death, although he does not understand that it was at his uncle's instigation. By Act V Scene 4, he has already become the new duke, despite his youth. His response to overhearing Flamineo's insulting remarks behind his back, that he has known 'a poor woman's bastard better favoured' (V.4.2), and to his face, that he should 'be merry' since he has now inherited the dukedom, merits the just reproach to 'Study your prayer, sir, and be penitent' (V.4.20). He subsequently forbids Flamineo's presence. The audience are likely to approve of this behaviour since we have seen what a malevolent influence Flamineo is and how dangerous to all around him. Nevertheless when at the end, as the new duke, Giovanni speaks the final words of the play and is responsible for the restoration of order, the audience are bound to have misgivings on account of his immaturity and likely dependence upon his uncle, Francisco.

THEMES

LOVE AND DEATH

The eminent Webster scholar Charles Forker asserts that:

> Although the love-death nexus amounted to something of a cultural obsession in the early seventeenth century and was variously employed by many Renaissance dramatists, Webster seems to have been especially drawn to the motif, touching upon it both early and late and exploring its potentialities most profoundly in the three unaided plays that constitute his finest and most distinctive achievement (*Skull Beneath the Skin: The Achievement of John Webster*, Southern Illinois UP, 1986, p. 237).

The love of Brachiano for Vittoria provides the main impetus for the plot of *The White Devil*. The play suggests that love is an anarchic force which destroys the established social order, disrupting the institution of marriage and the political alliances which it has cemented, as well as the personal lives of all those caught up in it. Its inevitable outcome is death; within the play's terms love and death are indissoluble, parasitically intertwined in Francisco's formula, 'Like mistletoe on sere elms spent by weather' (II.1.396). All those who love in *The White Devil* die as a result of love: the love of Brachiano and Vittoria signifies the death of Isabella and Camillo and the revenge of their deaths leads directly to the deaths of Brachiano and Vittoria themselves. The play explores the nature of love and the social structures which direct it in ways which turn it into the destructive force we see.

The love of Brachiano and Vittoria is adulterous and therefore illicit, which calls into question ideas concerning the institution of marriage in the period. It was essentially a system designed to ensure patrilineal inheritance (that is the legitimate continuation of the male bloodline) and establish political alliances in which women in particular functioned as useful pawns. As Dena Goldberg explains this was the norm amongst the European aristocracy of the period:

CHECK THE BOOK

Charles R. Forker's *Skull Beneath the Skin: The Achievement of John Webster* (1986) is the most significant and important critical biography of Webster.

CHECK THE BOOK

There is little sense that this is a 'love story' in the way that the youthful tragedy of *Romeo and Juliet* is, although it could be argued that in some ways *The White Devil* resembles Shakespeare's later tragedy of love, *Antony and Cleopatra*, which features an adulterous middle-aged couple whose love destroys an empire.

LOVE AND DEATH continued

QUESTION

How far do you agree with Dena Goldberg that 'The tragic paradox of her [Vittoria's] life is that her magnificent life force can only express itself in death – in the murder of the two people who stand in the way of marriage with Brachiano, and consequently, in her own destruction' (*Between Worlds: A Study of the Plays of John Webster*, 1987, p. 23)?

She is the victim of a marriage arranged by her family in a futile effort to reverse the trend of economic decline initiated by a spendthrift father. The strong implicit critique of arranged marriages is reinforced by the fact that Vittoria's lover, the Duke of Brachiano, is similarly trapped in a politically advantageous marriage to the sister of Francisco de Medicis. (*Between Worlds: A Study of the Plays of John Webster*, Wilfrid Laurier UP, 1987, p. 22)

Despite the adulterous nature of the relationship the audience's sympathy is likely to be with the lovers since it is clear from the start that, as Goldberg puts it, 'The marriage between this charming, knowledgeable, high-spirited woman and the silly, impotent Camillo has (in Jacobean terms) offended the natural order' (pp. 22–3).

The cost of achieving personal fulfilment is enormous, though. As Cornelia, Vittoria's mother, makes clear such a union is regarded as a sin and will lead to social and moral condemnation, 'If thou dishonour thus thy husband's bed, / Be thy life short as are the funeral tears / In great men's' (I.2.293–5). Disturbingly, the audience has already witnessed how within thirty lines of Brachiano and Vittoria being alone together, she is confiding her dream of the death of her husband and his wife.

One of the play's cruellest **ironies** is the way in which Isabella's death is brought about not simply by her husband's love for another woman but specifically by her love for him as she kisses his portrait three times, according to the detailed stage directions of the **dumb show**:

> … *she kneels down as to prayers, then draws the curtain of the picture, does three reverences to it, and kisses it thrice.* (II.2.23)

The manner of her death and Brachiano's heartless commentary 'Excellent, then she's dead' (II.2.24) is a grotesque betrayal of her love, but perhaps there is a suggestion that the nature of her love is misguided, sacrilegious even, by turning her husband's image into an icon of adoration. Her death is avenged in turn by Lodovico who proclaims to Monticelso his own love for Isabella as a motive, 'Sir I did love Brachiano's Duchess dearly;' (IV.3.112). Likewise

Flamineo's 'love' for Zanche, however constrained he claims it is, leads directly to the death of his brother, Marcello.

The play also examines the maternal love of Cornelia and Isabella. Both women, Webster makes a point of stating, unusually for the time, suckled their own children, demonstrating the strength of their maternal love. They both suffered at the hands of selfish husbands. Isabella is killed by her love for her husband while Cornelia is ultimately destroyed by her love for her children. When Flamineo kills his brother, Marcello, she attempts to protect him by lying, fearing to lose him as well, 'One arrow's grazed already; it were vain / T'lose this: for that will ne'er be found again' (V.2.69–70). As a result, Cornelia loses her mind but it is through watching his mother performing the funeral rites for his brother that Flamineo finally experiences an emotion akin to love: 'Compassion' (V.4.112). Giovanni undoubtedly loved his mother as Francisco records, 'Thou didst love her' (III.2.334) after the child's heartrending account of her death. It remains to be seen whether his love for his father leads him to avenge his death in turn.

Sibling love is a complicated emotion, sometimes dangerous and problematic. In Webster's other great **tragedy**, *The Duchess of Malfi*, the jealous, incestuous desire of her brother Ferdinand is a motivating factor in the duchess's death. Any such emotion is much less obvious in this play although Gale Edwards's 1996 Royal Shakespeare Company's production emphasised Flamineo's erotic desire for his sister. In another example of sibling affection, Isabella goes to her brother, Francisco, to complain of her husband's infidelity. The revenge he exacts for her death is motivated by a mixture of his sense of family honour and pride and love for his sister, as he tells Monticelso: 'Believe me I am nothing but her grave, / and I shall keep her blessed memory / Longer than a thousand epitaphs' (III.2.340–2). His first **ironic** step is to compose a letter to Vittoria 'I am in love, / In love with Corombona' (IV.1.119–20) which chillingly highlights the casual meaninglessness of the term and how it can be hijacked for hideous and inappropriate ends.

If love inevitably leads to death then sometimes, the play suggests, at the final extremity as the protagonists face their deaths, death can, paradoxically, lead in turn back to love. Brachiano's death from the

**CHECK
THE BOOK**

Lawrence Stone's *The Family, Sex and Marriage in England 1500–1800* (1977) details changing social mores in the period in which marriage gradually became less a financial and political alliance and more a relationship based on companionship and the personal inclination of the individuals involved.

CONTEXT

Lodovico's ingenious plan to anoint the pommel of Brachiano's saddle with poison (V.1.70) echoes the plot of the Catholic conspirator Edward Squire who was hanged in 1598 for attempting to assassinate Elizabeth I in this way.

poisoned beaver is horrible. The **irony** of the poison touching his lips is clear and his death not undeserved but his final anguished cries 'Vittoria! Vittoria!' (V.3.171) speak of his love for this woman who, as he proclaimed at the start would become everything to him: 'you shall to me at once / Be dukedom, health, wife, children, friends, and all' (I.2.265–6). Throughout the play Flamineo has ruthlessly exploited his sister in order to advance his own prospects. As he admits to his brother: 'I made a kind of path / To her and mine own preferment' (III.1.34–5). In the final act he tests her love for him and she fails spectacularly. Presumably if she had kept her side of the suicide pact, he would have happily allowed her to die. It is not until both are truly facing death at the hands of the conspirators that Flamineo, in admiration of her proud spirit, confesses, 'Th'art a noble sister — / I love thee now' (V.6.239–40).

IDENTITY AND DISGUISE

As the discussion of characterisation revealed, identity is a problematic notion in *The White Devil*, never fixed or stable. It is hard to say exactly who or what each of the characters is or represents; they are **ambiguous**, shifting their positions and open to radically different interpretations. In the course of the play each of the characters changes, playing a number of different roles, many adopting disguises of one sort or another to achieve their ends; Francisco, for example, is the righteously-indignant, concerned brother in Act II Scene 1, a moralist in Act III during the arraignment, a scheming Machiavellian in Act IV, finally disguising himself as the moor, Mulinassar, in Act V in order to avenge Isabella's death; Lodovico, the ruined nobleman, turns ruthless assassin, and adopts the disguise of a Capuchin monk in order to carry out this revenge. In the course of the play Brachiano is in turn besotted courtly wooer, genial father, cruel husband, ruthless murderer, jealous lover, vicious tyrant, and fearful murder victim.

All the characters play different roles at different times, even the virtuous Isabella play-acts the 'fury' to fool her brother and keep the peace. Monticelso wears scarlet as a cardinal but, after his election as pope, he puts on white papal robes creating a deeper form of disguise for his villainy. Flamineo himself is the most consistently mercurial character, constant in his changeability, a self-seeking materialist and cold-hearted manipulator, he plays the concerned brother-in-law to Camillo in order to make him a cuckold and then to kill him; most notably he play-acts his own death in the final act to test Vittoria.

The effect of such rapid changes in each of the characters is to increase the audience's sense of disorientation, making it difficult to fix on any one idea about the play and its characters, and is undoubtedly one of the factors responsible for its mixed critical reception over the years. The audience may well feel at times that like Flamineo that they are 'in a mist' (V.6.258). It would be possible to suggest, as earlier critics did, that Webster was simply not good at characterisation; alternatively the audience/reader might conclude that this technique is deliberately designed to pose questions about the meaning of identity and the purposes of theatre and disguise. In his study of Webster and fellow playwright, John Ford (who was greatly influenced by Webster), Rowland Wymer suggests that this instability of identity is a deliberate strategy on Webster's part:

> So many of the minor characters, despite the limited nature of their parts, behave in unexpected and contradictory ways that one is justified in assuming that a general principle of characterisation ... is in operation (*Webster and Ford,* St Martin's Press, 1995, p. 43).

In *Radical Tragedy* (Harvester Wheatsheaf, 1984), Jonathan Dollimore interprets this instability of identity as an effect of politics. Dollimore argues (p. 231), that the lack of fixed identity in Jacobean plays such as Webster's signifies the psychological response of individuals to the social dislocation of the changing times in which Webster and his peers were writing (see **Part Five: Historical background**). In other words, Webster's technique of characterisation in the play seems deliberate, in that he sees character not as an essential quality relating to any deep sense of interior being but as fluid and provisional, responding to circumstance and situation, adopting different roles and disguises.

POLITICS AND RELIGION

In drama the personal is inevitably more engaging than the political. The audience become involved with the characters at an emotional level. Nevertheless, right from the start it is apparent that *The White Devil* is deeply concerned with political matters and with the

CONTEXT

John Ford was eight years younger than Webster but they knew each other most likely through the Middle Temple. They collaborated on plays such as the lost *Keep the Widow Waking*. Ford became an important playwright in the Caroline theatre (that is, during the reign of Charles I). His best-known plays are *'Tis Pity She's a Whore* (1629–33) and *The Broken Heart* (1625–33).

political role of religion. At this time Italy was a collection of city-states such as Venice, Florence and Padua, which were ruled by feudal aristocrats – Brachiano rules Padua as Francisco rules Florence. Rome was the centre of the Papal States of which the Pope was head. The Church had wide legal powers and its jurisdiction covered civil as well as religious and spiritual matters based on its expertise in interpreting Canon law, which later became the basis of Civil law.

In the very first scene, Lodovico complains that he is being punished because he has 'great enemies' (I.1.7) who can get away with their crimes because of their political power. Lodovico is not necessarily a reliable witness nor is Flamineo, who complains of the same thing. The development of the play, however, reveals that this is the case: that the powerful and wealthy are able to do as they please without taking account of the law. This inequality before the law, the play suggests, produces a deeply flawed, corrupt society. The alliance between Monticelso and Francisco against Brachiano represents the alliance between Church and State with the two parties working together to further their own interests. Monticelso is seen as a ruthless power-broker motivated by the desire for personal revenge and with a personal interest in the estate of his nephew, Camillo. Judges at this time were not impartial arbiters but operated an inquisitorial system in which they were free to accuse defendants who, like Vittoria, had little defence but their wits. Complaints of legal corruption were frequent but in practice there was little redress.

The play demonstrates how the corrupt political system affects the whole social structure. The only way in which those without power or wealth can hope to further their careers is through serving one of these so-called nobles in whatever nefarious way possible, 'Knaves do grow great by being great men's apes' (IV.2.243). It also questions the role of religion at a structural level, featuring **parodies** of the Church sacraments of marriage, confession and death in Brachiano's divorce of Isabella, which literally reverses the marriage service, Monticelso's 'confession' of Lodovico (IV.3.81–128), and Lodovico and Gasparo's blasphemous mock '*Commendatio Animae*' at the death of Brachiano (V.3.132–70).

> **CONTEXT**
>
> Early modern society was highly litigious, that is people went to law frequently, although corruption amongst lawyers was notorious. Francis Bacon, Viscount St Alban, was dismissed from the post of Lord Chancellor for taking bribes, although he later claimed that he had pleaded guilty in order to save King James I from embarrassment.

Religion is responsible for formulating and upholding the basic moral tenets of society. When those in charge of the institution are corrupt then the whole of society is blighted. The most pious characters are Cornelia and Isabella, who are both destroyed in the course of the play. The corruption of the institutions which hold political power and control the state, in this case the Church and the law, leads to the disintegration of all social bonds, of individual characters, families and the whole of society, which Ralph Berry describes as 'a depiction of a disintegrating world order' (*The Art of John Webster*, Clarendon Press, 1972, p. 78). The play was written thirty years before the outbreak of civil war in England but the constitutional issues which led to this event were already subject to debate; Jacobean and Caroline drama provided one possible site for exploring such issues.

LANGUAGE

STYLE AND TONE

The language in *The White Devil* is a mixture of verse and prose. The verse is principally **iambic pentameter**. While Webster has often been praised for the beauty of his verse, in which he has been judged 'a good second' to Shakespeare (by the poet Swinburne) some critics have been disturbed and puzzled by the tone of much of the play's language. Despite the dark subject-matter and tragic events depicted, the tone is frequently **ironic and satirical**, especially in Flamineo's cynical commentaries. Critics have tried to account for this in various ways; Travis Bogard argues that Webster has deliberately blended 'two almost incompatible genres, tragedy and satire' which he calls 'tragic satire' (*The Tragic Satire of John Webster*, Russell and Russell, 1965, p. ix) while Jacqueline Pearson believes that 'The play is a tragedy which reaches its final statement through the language and forms of comedy and tragicomedy' (*Tragedy and tragicomedy in the plays of John Webster*, Manchester UP, 1980, p. 53).

The changes in tone are rapid and frequent. In Act I Scene 2, there is comedy over hiding the duke in a cupboard and in the tricking of Camillo: 'Some trick now must be thought on to divide / My brother-in-law from his fair bedfellow.' (I.2.35–8), while Flamineo

QUESTION

How important are the comic aspects of the play, and what purpose do they serve?

persuades his sister with promises of erotic delight, almost cloying in their intensity:

> Thou shalt lie in a bed stuffed with turtles' feathers, swoon in perfumed linen like the fellow was smothered in roses, so perfect shall be thy happiness, that as men at sea think land and trees and ships go that way they go, so both heaven and earth shall seem to go your voyage. Shalt meet him, 'tis fixed, with nails of diamonds to inevitable necessity. (I.2.152–8)

Here Webster employs prose but in a particularly poetic style, using a profusion of exotic images and **similes**, while Brachiano addresses Vittoria in the hyperbole associated with the Petrarchan sonnet and **courtly love**:

> Excellent creature.
> We call the cruel fair, what name for you
> That are so merciful. (I.2.212–14)

In a further switch of language and tone, within a dozen lines Vittoria is confiding her dark, melancholy dream (I.2.231–9), shortly followed by Cornelia's doom-laden warning, 'Woe to light hearts, they still forerun our fall' (I.2.267) and Flamineo's angry response: 'What fury raised thee up?' (I.2.268). Thus the scene runs the gamut of styles and tones within three hundred and fifty lines.

In her arraignment in Act III Vittoria is capable of heroic poetry as she defies Cardinal Monticelso in ringing tones:

> It shall not be a house of convertites.
> My mind shall make it honester to me
> Than the Pope's palace, and more peaceable
> Than thy soul, though thou art a cardinal. (III.2.289–94)

Cornelia's question to Flamineo in her grief, 'You are, I take it, the gravemaker' (V.4.78) is bitterly **ironic** in the circumstances while her dirge for her dead son is full of **pathos**:

> 'Call for the robin-red-breast and the wren,
> Since o'er shady groves they hover,

And with leaves and flowers do cover
The friendless bodies of unburied men. (V.4.92–101)

The final scene, in particular, runs through the whole range of emotions and changes in tone and style, including **comedy**, **satire**, **melodrama** and **tragedy**, causing the audience to experience a bewildering mix of conflicting thoughts and emotions.

Running alongside these spectacular stylistic fireworks and quick-changes are a whole set of short sayings, one- and sometimes two-liners, which encapsulate pithy moral maxims known as *sententiae*. They are sometimes in Latin but often in English, and usually signalled in the text by quotation marks, for example, Isabella's '"Unkindness do thy office, poor heart break, / Those are the killing griefs which dare not speak"' (II.1.276–7) or Flamineo's 'We think caged birds sing, when indeed they cry' (V.4.120) or Vittoria's final 'O happy they that never saw the court, / "Nor ever knew great man but by report"' (V.6.259–60). Their use was common in Senecan tragedy (see **Part Five: Literary background**), which was so influential on Elizabethan and Jacobean drama. Critics however are divided about their presence in Webster; some arguing that their use represents a weakness in his writing. Ian Jack for example believes that:

> Webster's ... plays contain brilliant patches of poetry – they appear whenever he touches on the small area which acted as his inspiration – but lack imaginative coherence ... this attempt to shore up chaos with a sententious philosophy is a flagrant artistic insincerity ('The Case of John Webster', *Scrutiny*, vol. 16, 1949, reprinted in *John Webster: A Critical Anthology*, 1969, pp. 157–64, p. 159).

Jacqueline Pearson, however, suggests that the short sayings were:

> ... a source of pleasure to Webster's first audiences, and even today the *sententia* can obtain fine dramatic results. Sententious statements as Webster uses them are direct comments on the action, and serve as agents of the satire. They represent the dramatist's point of view by making a generalised statement to point the significance of a speech or scene (*Tragedy and tragicomedy in the plays of John Webster*, 1980, p. 102).

CHECK THE BOOK

Flamineo's comment 'We think caged birds sing, when indeed they cry' (V.4.120) refers to a proverb already well-known by Webster's time. The sentiment has been echoed down the centuries including by the American poet Paul Laurence Dunbar whose poem, *Sympathy* starts 'I know why the caged bird sings, ah me'. Maya Angelou used this for the title of the first part of her autobiography, *I Know Why the Caged Bird Sings* (1969) describing the difficulties of a young black woman growing up in the racist society of the American south.

CONTEXT

Bertolt Brecht (1889–1956) was a German playwright and director. A life-long Marxist, he developed a radical theory of theatre known as *verfremdungseffekt* (usually translated as an alienating or distancing effect) designed to break down the idea of theatre as reality by highlighting its representational quality and reminding the audience that it was watching a performance. It was to prove highly influential in twentieth century drama. His most famous works are *The Threepenny Opera, Mother Courage and Her Children* and *The Caucasian Chalk Circle*.

Ralph Berry (*The Art of John Webster,* Clarendon Press, 1972) also thinks they signal a 'lack of integration', that *sententiae* exist as 'fragments of an older morality' and that their use 'entails an almost stylistic shift, from informal to formal' which have a 'jarring' effect on the audience, akin to modern theories of the 'alienation effect' of Bertolt Brecht. He goes on to argue, though, that this effect is deliberate and that, 'they fulfil, in diffused form, the function of the chorus' (p. 77). In Greek classical drama, the chorus were a group of characters who were essentially spectators rather than actors within the drama, and who spoke to the audience as well as the characters and commented on the action of the play. You may have noted how in his address 'To the Reader', Webster defends his play for its lack of a '*sententious Chorus*' (p. 20). Berry is arguing that Webster has appropriated this function to these moral maxims or *sententiae* and incorporated them into his play-text, distributing them between the characters and forming a moral framework for the chaos of events.

IMAGERY AND ALLUSION

In his address 'To the Reader' Webster accepts that he was 'a long time in finishing this tragedy' (p. 21). The fact that he wrote slowly and carefully, without 'a goose-quill, winged with two feathers', (p. 21) may in part explain the play's dense texture in which verbal and visual images and **allusions** pile up on top of each other. Certain images are repeated throughout the play: iconographic use of black and white, **metaphors** and **similes** relating to animals, vegetation, disease, parasitism and painting; each of these is played on and reworked insistently across the text often producing **ironic** counterpoints as when Gasparo tells Lodovico:

> Your followers
> Have swallowed you like mummia, and …
> Vomit you up i'th'kennel— (I.1.15–18)

only to find the image recurring in Isabella's terrible fury against Vittoria, 'Preserve her flesh like mummia, for trophies / Of my just anger' (II.1.248–9). Or when Monticelso invites Francisco to share his thoughts on Isabella's death, 'Come, come my lord, untie your folded thoughts, / And let them dangle loose as a bride's hair' (IV.1.1–2) which precisely prefigures Vittoria's appearance at the opening to Act V.

Black and white are so central to the play, as the title suggests, as to function thematically. The symbol or image of the white devil has many possible interpretations – varying from the specific (perhaps referring to a single character such as Vittoria), to the general (an all-pervading sense of evil in the play). In terms of the origins of the phrase, the devil was traditionally regarded as black so the 'white devil' of the title suggests a creature black on the inside but white outside. 'The white devil is worse than the black' was a proverbial saying signifying a hypocrite. The origin of the concept is biblical, from Jesus's warnings about hypocrites,

> Woe unto you, scribes and Pharisees, hypocrites! For ye are like unto whited sepulchres, which indeed appear beautiful outward, but are within full of dead men's bones, and of all uncleanness. (Matthew 23:27)

and St Paul's attack on the appearance of false apostles:

> For such men are false apostles, deceitful workmen, masquerading as apostles of Christ. And no wonder, for Satan himself masquerades as an angel of light. It is not surprising, then, if his servants masquerade as servants of righteousness. Their end will be what their actions deserve. (II Corinthians 11:13–15)

Webster plays with the idea of the contrast between black and white, appearance and reality, undermining conventional distinctions between good and evil. Apart from the Moorish maid, Zanche, there are two more 'black' characters, Francisco during Act V when in disguise as the Moor Mulinassar, as well as the non-speaking part of 'Jacques, a Moor, servant to Giovanni'. In Act II Scene 1, 'little Jacques the Moor' (**s.d.**) does not speak but he enters with 'young Giovanni' creating a strong visual effect. Two characters who wear white are Monticelso after his election as pope and Vittoria for her wedding. Black and white are used emblematically throughout and verbal references to Vittoria, in particular, highlight her affinity with whiteness and light. In the final scene, though, she confronts the darkness within as she confesses: 'My soul, like to a ship in a black storm, / is driven I know not whither' (V.6.246–7) to which Flamineo responds: 'Then

---

CONTEXT

The image of the soul as a ship at sea is derived from St Paul's letter to the Hebrews (6:19–20) which talks about 'hope' as the 'anchor of the soul'. Vittoria's words imply therefore that she is without hope of salvation.

cast anchor, / Prosperity doth bewitch men seeming clear, / But seas do laugh, show white when rocks are near' (V.6.249–51). Just before he dies Flamineo himself confesses, 'My life was a black charnel' (V.6.270).

There are over a hundred examples of animal **imagery** in *The White Devil*. Such constant usage represents a systematic process of human degradation, likening men to wolves, birds, a maggot and so on. Webster builds up speeches with complex sets of images as when Monticelso berates Brachiano:

> When you awake from this lascivious dream,
> Repentance then will follow, like the sting
> Placed in the adder's tail. (II.1.35–8)

His speech goes on to cover vegetation, symbols of power, jewels, destruction and natural disaster (II.1.39–42). The overall effect is of pessimism and decay, and the sense that nature itself is somehow corrupt.

Webster's dense writing texture is also created in part by his literary allusions and borrowings from other writers. In his Introduction to *John Webster's Borrowing*, R. W. Dent argues that 'We already know for certain that the extent of Webster's borrowings was extraordinary even for the age in which he wrote' (Cambridge UP, 1961, p. 221). This reworking of other writers' phrases and images formed an important part of contemporary writing practices. It was known as 'imitation' and specifically recommended by the humanist teaching in the grammar schools and universities. As Hereward T. Price explains though, Webster:

> … notoriously lifted his images from a large number of writers, especially from Sidney and from Montaigne. But it is also true that he rarely borrows without improving on his source. His mind was a sieve through which only the essential elements passed. He trims his borrowings so closely as to achieve the utmost economy and sharpness of phrase … whatever he took he worked into the essential substance of the play. ('The Function of Imagery in Webster', *P.M.L.A.*, vol. 70, September 1955, reprinted in *John Webster: A Critical Anthology*, 1969, pp. 176–202, p. 178)

CONTEXT

In his *Defence of Poesy* or *Apology for Poetry* (1595), Sir Philip Sidney says 'Poesy therefore is an art of imitation, for so Aristotle termeth it in his word *mimesis*, that is to say, a representing, counterfeiting, or figuring forth – to speak metaphorically, a speaking picture – with this end, to teach and delight.' Humanist scholars thought that the best way of learning to write well was to copy the style and ideas from classical models.

Dent demonstrates how carefully Webster was able to integrate other writers' ideas and images into his text, making them his own:

WHITE DEVIL	SOURCE OF IMAGE/OTHER WRITERS
MONTICELSO: Well, well, such counterfeit jewels Make true ones oft suspected.	More: 'many well counterfeited jewels make the true mistrusted.'
VITTORIA: You are deceived; For know that all your strict-combined heads Which strike against this mine of diamonds, Shall prove but glassen hammers, they shall break, – These are but feigned shadows of my evils.	Matthieu: 'those heads which shall strike against this rock of diamant will prove glass.'
Terrify babes, my lord, with painted devils, I am past such needless palsy — for your names Of whore and murd'ress they proceed from you,	Shakespeare: ''tis the eye of childhood / That fears a painted devil.'
As if a man should spit against the wind, The filth returns in's face.	Yver: 'Thou shalt be like him that spitteth against the wind, whose slaver fleeth in his own face.'

This is only one of many such passages which demonstrate how carefully Webster was able to build up the texture of his writing by incorporating ideas and images from other writers. This is not to be confused with the concept of plagiarism. As with the *sententiae* discussed above Webster would probably have expected readers to recognise many of these images and for such recognition to increase their pleasure and appreciation of his work.

> **CONTEXT**
>
> Plagiarism, that is passing off someone else's ideas or work as your own and which we are now so concerned about, is a concept we have inherited from early modern times when writing entered the commercial market-place for the first time and authors claimed intellectual property rights over their work.

LATIN, INKHORN TERMS AND PLAIN SPEAKING

Early modern drama featured the use of other languages surprisingly often onstage – for example Shakespeare's *Henry IV Part 1* has a Welsh Princess who speaks no English, and *Henry V* a French one with a scene in French; Dekker's *Shoemaker's Holiday* features a Dutch sea captain while Middleton's *A Chaste Maid in Cheapside* uses cod-Latin and a Welsh lady who sings. These may reflect the cosmopolitan nature of the capital at this time but it is clear that playwrights were not afraid to write short sequences in foreign tongues. The amount of Latin in *The White Devil* is notable though. Most of it is related to the ceremonies of the Catholic Church, for example in Act IV Scene 3 when Monticelso is elected pope. There is also the horrific **parodic** inversion of the *Commendatio animae* by Lodovico and Gasparo disguised as Capuchin monks at Brachiano's deathbed in Act V Scene 3. Apart from these specific instances there are a number of *sententiae* in Latin sprinkled throughout the text such as Francisco's '*Flectere si nequeo superos, Acheronta movebo*' (IV.1.138) which means 'If I cannot prevail upon the gods above, I will move the gods of the infernal regions' and is from Virgil's *Aeneid* VII, 312. The point in the play in which the use of Latin is foregrounded though is Vittoria's arraignment in Act III Scene 2 when she objects to its use in court, 'I will not have my accusation clouded / In a strange tongue:' (III.2.18–19). This objection on her part is clearly designed to win the assent and sympathy of the audience both onstage and offstage and is bound to raise further questions about the use of Latin in the rest of the play and the extent to which it is designed to induce fear and mystify.

Vittoria's next objection is to the Lawyer's verbose use of legal jargon. Such complicated Latinate words and phrases were known as 'inkhorn terms'. Such a style was specifically associated with Roman Catholicism so Vittoria is making a religious and political point in her objection. Monticelso takes over the role of her accuser and although claiming that he will be 'plainer with you, and paint out / Your follies in more natural red and white / Than that upon your cheek' (III.2.51–3), he addresses her in a style full of rhetorical figures. Vittoria replies using the straightforward 'plain style' which wins her the sympathy of the audience (and which was associated with Protestantism) and produces that conviction of her innocence, even though we know that she is guilty.

DRAMATIC TECHNIQUES

SPECTACLE

When reading a play on the page, it is not easy to get an idea of just how spectacular a play like *The White Devil* can be in production with its processions, fights, **dumb shows**, ghosts, trial, masques and madness. On the public stage for which this play was written there was little in the way of scenery or properties but Webster creates spectacular visual effects by formal set-piece displays in procession or combats. These he alternates with smaller private scenes in order to create visual patterns.

One of the most important ways in which Webster's audience was impressed and entertained was through the use of lavish costume, as the diary of Philip Henslowe, the theatrical entrepreneur, reveals, the most expensive element of any play. Colour was used **symbolically** and costume observed the decorum of Tudor sumptuary laws which laid down colour, style and fabric appropriate as a mark of social status. As Andrew Gurr explains 'Costume was an instrument of meaning as well as spectacle and colour' (*The Shakespearean Stage 1574–1642*, Cambridge UP, 1992, p. 194) and the audience familiar with the rules were able to 'read' a character's costume. The use of colour symbolism is notable in *The White Devil*, not only in Vittoria's bridal white and Monticelso's cardinal's scarlet and subsequently papal white, but in the magnificent costumes of the various military orders worn by the Ambassadors and described by Lodovico in Act IV Scene 3.

Webster writes scenes with large spectacular processions, such as Act I Scene 2, when Brachiano is accompanied by a retinue with lights and torches, which is then suddenly ordered away. The following scene repeats the process when Brachiano arrives to visit Francisco, who instantly orders 'Void the chamber' (II.1.19). The finely-dressed Ambassadors process across the stage before Vittoria's arraignment (III.1.62–76). Her trial represents a scene of dramatic visual as well as verbal conflict. The Ambassadors process again in the garb of their military orders in Act IV Scene 3 before the announcement of Monticelso's election and entry – '*in state*' meaning with all due ceremony. Vittoria and Brachiano's wedding

CHECK THE FILM

The *Diary* of Philip Henslowe (c.1550–1616), the theatrical entrepreneur and impresario, basically an account book, is nevertheless one of the most valuable and important sources of information for theatrical practices in the period. Henslowe was played by Geoffrey Rush in the film *Shakespeare in Love* (1998).

CONTEXT

The Order of the Annunciation, founded in 1362 by Amadeus of Savoy, wore white satin with a purple velvet cloak and gold collar; the Order of the Garter founded in 1350 by Edward III in England wore a purple velvet mantle over a crimson velvet gown, a gold chain with white roses and a garter in gold, pearl and precious stones.

SPECTACLE continued

CHECK THE NET

For details of Elizabethan fencing and swordplay go to: **www. elizabethan-era.org. uk** and click on 'Elizabethan Sports'.

CHECK THE FILM

There have been a number of films of *Hamlet* including Laurence Olivier's brooding black and white version (1948), Franco Zeffirelli's 1990 version starring Mel Gibson and Glenn Close, Kenneth Branagh's 1996 version set in Regency costume and shot at Blenheim Palace and Michael Almereyda's with Ethan Hawke as Hamlet (2000). This updated the story to modern day Manhattan where corrupt grey 'suits' run the Denmark Corporation in a spiritual landscape of urban isolation and the play-within-a play is a home-made video.

procession opens the fifth act and Francisco and the conspirators enter disguised some forty lines later. Act V Scene 3 opens with the fighting 'at barriers'. Ability at sword fighting was one of an actor's necessary accomplishments and watching staged battles or, as here, a tournament, was an important part of the entertainment. The final act is full of movement and spectacle, much of it of a lurid sensational nature interspersed with moments of **pathos**, as in Cornelia's winding of her dead son's corpse, set at the back of the stage in the so-called discovery space (see **Detailed summaries**, Act V Scene 4).

DUMB SHOW

Webster includes not one but two **dumb shows** in *The White Devil*. They occur one after the other in Act II Scene 2. This dramatic device of silent pantomimed actions derived from medieval theatre and was old-fashioned by 1612. The most famous example comes at the start of the play-within-a-play in Shakespeare's *Hamlet*. However, Webster's dumb shows fulfil different functions from Hamlet's desire to 'catch the conscience of the king' through re-enacting an event from the past. Firstly they are economical of time and space, enabling the audience to witness for themselves the deaths of both Isabella and Camillo in rapid succession. More significantly they are framed by the voyeurism of Brachiano and the Conjuror who reveals them to the duke through his particular art; the audience is therefore able to witness Brachiano's response to the two events. The effect is to distance us from the murders themselves, which were 'performed' in the 'discovery space' at the back of the stage, causing us to focus instead on the reactions of the man who ordered both murders. The two deaths are very different both in their mode of operation, appropriate to the character of the victims, and in the effect they are likely to have on the audience. As Kate Aughterson suggests:

> The dumb shows are the first direct visual intimation of the actual dark deeds which propel the play, and much of its imagery. Their silent delivery reinforces our sense of the claustrophobic, self-interested political world that is propelled by inner desires and demons which remain hidden by the surface world of courtiers and politics. Finally, the ritualistic representation of

death enhances the horror of the action, a horror reinforced by the framing. (*Webster: The Tragedies*, Palgrave, 2001, p. 167)

There is a ludicrous incongruity in the way in which Brachiano puts on the Conjuror's special 'charmed' 'night-cap' in order to witness 'The circumstance that breaks your Duchess' heart' (II.2.23). The horror of her death contrasts with the laughter of Doctor Julio and Christophero, Isabella's suffering, and her son's grief in comparison with Brachiano's self-satisfied response, 'Excellent, then she's dead' (II.2.24). The death of Camillo, by contrast, is undignified, in a busy scene full of activity. The final events as Flamineo and Marcello are detained and the guards go to arrest Vittoria prepare the audience for the next act and Vittoria's arraignment.

SOLILOQUY AND ASIDES

Soliloquy, that is a single character onstage talking to him or herself, was a typical theatrical device of the time, designed to allow the audience private access to a character's thoughts – again the most well-known example is Hamlet in speeches such as 'To be or not to be'. In the absence of other characters onstage, such speeches are directed straight to the audience, thus enabling the character to build up a relationship with the audience, a procedure which tends to make even villains sympathetic and invites audience collusion. Many of these features stem from the role of the Vice in medieval morality plays who was often an allegorical representation of one of the seven deadly sins. A comic role, the Vice typically tempted the hero to evil-doing, taking the audience into his confidence and revealing his plans in advance in soliloquies. Shakespearean characters who derive from the tradition are Iago in *Othello* and Richard in *Richard III*. It is always revealing to see which characters are given soliloquies and consider why this should be and the effect it has on how the audience responds to them.

In *The White Devil* Webster uses the device sparingly but effectively, divided between important characters. Flamineo has a brief one at the end of Act I, just after his mother's exit, in which he confides his plans to the audience: 'We are engaged to mischief and must on' (I.2.345) and that the path chosen is to be devious, 'winding and indirect' (I.2.352). He has another in Act V Scene 5, after seeing his mother perform his brother's funeral rites.

 CHECK THE BOOK

Another very famous soliloquy from the time appears in Act I Scene 1 of Shakespeare's *Richard III*. The lines, spoken sarcastically by Richard as he plots the downfall of his enemies, are one of the most enduring beginnings to any play: 'Now is the winter of our discontent / Made glorious summer by this son of York.'

Francisco has a short one and a longer one in Act IV Scene 1 (lines 37–42 and lines 76–138) in which Monticelso tries to persuade him to avenge the death of Isabella. Lodovico is given one at the end of Act IV Scene 3 (lines 141–53). The otherwise insignificant Hortensio has a short **soliloquy** at the end of Act V Scene 5 (lines 12–15). The purpose in each case is to tell the audience what is going to happen. More importantly they learn why. Each of the villains reflects on their situation and then makes a conscious, informed decision about the course of action they will pursue. In other words they choose evil knowingly. This thrusts the moral onus onto the audience, who are invited to share the characters' intimate thoughts and follow the thinking which leads up to their decisions. The audience will either be seduced and accede to the characters' reasoning and therefore implicitly collude in their course of action, or, by employing their critical faculties, will manage to distance themselves and refuse that position. Interestingly neither Vittoria nor Monticelso are given soliloquies.

 QUESTION

Does the fact that neither Vittoria nor Monticelso are given soliloquies affect audience response to these characters?

A related technique which Webster uses consistently is the **aside** in which characters speak onstage with others present but do not intend their words to be heard by all. Sometimes they direct their asides to other characters who are complicit in their schemes, for example in Act 1 Scene 2, when Flamineo and Vittoria plan to get rid of Camillo, or in Act V Scene 6 when Vittoria and Zanche try to outwit Flamineo. Since the audience overhear these remarks they, too, become confidants and accomplices. Sometimes asides are directed specifically to the audience who gain privileged information in that they are the only ones fully aware of what is happening, as for example after Isabella's furious tirade against Vittoria and her public rejection of Brachiano, she exits with an aside heard only by the audience, 'Unkindness do thy office, poor heart break, / Those are the killing griefs which dare not speak' (II.1.276–7). The audience are enabled a glimpse of the real thoughts and feelings of characters as well as the charade they put up in public. Again the effect is of distance and judgement. No character can be accepted at face value, and a degree of scepticism is engendered concerning their true motives.

THE PLAY ON THE STAGE

After its initial theatrical failure, *The White Devil* enjoyed success on the Jacobean and Caroline stage. It did not suit the tastes of the eighteenth or nineteenth centuries, though, and was not revived until 1925 when the Renaissance Theatre Company staged it in London. There was a further revival in 1935. It has been staged with greater regularity since the Second World War. A 1947 production starred Robert Helpmann as Flamineo and Margaret Rawlings as Vittoria. Helpmann's costume famously concealed a bag of sheep's intestines for the last act when Flamineo is stabbed by Lodovico. The National Theatre staged productions in 1969 and 1991, Michael Lindsay-Hogg directed it at the Old Vic in 1976 and Gale Edwards directed a production for the Royal Shakespeare Company in the Swan Theatre in 1996. Despite the considerable expense involved in its staging and the many challenges it presents a director, there have been numerous amateur and subsidised touring productions.

In *Text and Performance: The White Devil and The Duchess of Malfi* (Macmillan, 1988), Richard Allen Cave argues that given the difficulties both plays present:

> It is not surprising that the history of the tragedies in performance is not a wholly satisfying one. The problem is essentially one of style and discipline: a director has to find a way of realising on stage a specific 'period' sensibility but not to an extent where the detail becomes fussy and intrusive, getting in the way of an audience's imaginative engagement with the plays' metaphorical dimensions. (p. 42)

The White Devil's bold, modern-seeming mixture of styles and elements has encouraged directors to experiment with tone and setting. The National Theatre's 1969 production, directed by Frank Dunlop, had a permanent set which suggested crumbling stone walls which physically recreated the layout of an Elizabethan theatre. This allowed for a fluid playing-style. The set was in contrast to the costumes which were Renaissance designs made up in 'unusual modern fabrics' giving the impression of 'butterflies or moths'. Cave argues that 'The dominant image was of creatures mesmerised and all-too-quickly consumed by their own lusts like

QUESTION

If you were to stage a production of *The White Devil*, would you place it in a modern setting or a historical one? What alternative dimensions, or indeed problems, might a modern setting create?

the proverbial moth drawn to its extinction by the candle flame'
(p. 44). Lindsay Hogg's 1976 production at the Old Vic, by contrast,
updated the play, setting it in the lobby of a grand hotel. It was cool
and modern. In contrast to Geraldine McEwan's Vittoria in 1969,
the Venetian courtesan of Monticelso's accusation, Glenda Jackson
played her in 1976 as a modern feminist only too aware of her
oppression by **patriarchal** society in the shape of the Church and
society as well as husband, lover and brother. Philip Prowse's 1991
production at the National Theatre emphasised the play's **gothic**
elements in a claustrophobic set which reminded one critic of 'a
half-built crypt, or half-ruined mausoleum' (Benedict Nightingale,
The Times, 19 June 1991). Prowse made the decision to cast Vittoria,
Flamineo and Marcello as black, giving the production a
contemporary political resonance. The outstanding performance
was by common consent Josette Simon's complex, subtle Vittoria,
described by the critic Michael Coveney as 'a compelling,
languorously tragic portrait' (*Observer*, 23 June 1991).

The most successful recent production has undoubtedly been the
Royal Shakespeare Company's in 1996 directed by Gale Edwards:

> Edwards creates a sharply focused picture of Webster's post-
> Machiavellian world, supported by a batch of excellent
> performances. Here powerful men use morality as a cover for
> merciless pragmatism – a point exemplified by Stephen Boxer's
> chilly Duke of Florence; for women the only lever available to
> use against such men is sex. Jane Gurnett's Vittoria is fully aware
> both of the power sex gives her, and how fragile that power is.
> (Robert Hanks, *Independent*, 28 April 1996)

It was staged in the Swan theatre in Stratford-upon-Avon with a
simple set with three openings across the rear of the stage. Mood
was created by changes of light from bright red and gold for the
celebrations, to cold blues and greys for Isabella's death. The
production was much praised: 'such exuberant relish in the playing,
such economy with the externals' (David Murray, *Financial Times*,
29 April 1996). The intimate playing-space enhanced the ensemble
playing and allowed Richard McCabe to achieve a Flamineo 'of
startling depth' in a performance described as 'superbly louche' and
'funny' (Robert Hanks, *Independent*, 28 April 1996).

CHECK THE NET

For details of Gale Edwards's 1996 Royal Shakespeare Company production go to: **www.rsc.org.uk** and put 'White Devil' in the search box. Then click on 'Pictures and Exhibitions' and click on *The White Devil* picture on the right hand side.

PART FOUR

CRITICAL PERSPECTIVES

READING CRITICALLY

This section provides a range of critical viewpoints and perspectives on *The White Devil* and gives a broad overview of key debates, interpretations and theories proposed since the play was published. It is important to bear in mind the variety of interpretations and responses this text has produced, many of them shaped by the critics' own backgrounds and historical contexts.

No single view of the text should be seen as dominant – it is important that you arrive at your own judgements by questioning the perspectives described, and by developing your own critical insights. Objective analysis is a skill achieved through coupling close reading with an informed understanding of the key ideas, related texts and background information relevant to the text. These elements are all crucial in enabling you to assess the interpretations of other readers, and even to view works of criticism as texts in themselves. The ability to read critically will serve you well both in your study of the text, and in any critical writing, presentation, or further work you undertake.

ORIGINAL RECEPTION

The defensive tone of Webster's address 'To the Reader' suggests that the original reception of *The White Devil* was unfavourable or even hostile. Webster blames the weather, the theatre and the audience for its failure: 'It was acted in so dull a time of winter, presented in so open and black a theatre, that it wanted ... a full and understanding auditory' whereas he noted that 'most of the people that come to that playhouse, resemble ... ignorant asses' (p. 5). Despite the play's many spectacular effects and local references it must have presented the Red Bull audience with too much of a challenge for a wintry afternoon. It would have been better suited in every respect to the smaller, elite audiences of the indoor theatres. Rushing the play out in print the same year was an act of defiance,

 CHECK THE NET

The Red Bull was a seventeenth century London theatre in St John Street, Clerkenwell, which had been developed from an inn with a large square courtyard. For more information go to: **www.elizabethan-era.org.uk and click** on 'Elizabethan Theatres'.

CHECK THE BOOK

Samuel Pepys (1633–1703) was a talented and successful English naval administrator and MP but is chiefly remembered for his *Diary* which gives eyewitness accounts of many of the chief events of the Restoration period including the Great Fire of London (1666) as well as intimate details of his personal life and thoughts.

then, on Webster's part. His faith appears to have been justified since it was reprinted four times in the seventeenth century and each printing records a different acting venue. This suggests that, despite its disastrous opening, *The White Devil* went on to enjoy theatrical success and remained in the repertory until the closure of the theatres in 1642. The contemporary critic Henry Fitzjeffrey, writing in 1617, was however unimpressed, referring jeeringly to Webster as, 'crabbed Websterio, / The playwright-cartwright' and describing his work as 'so obscure / That none shall understand him' (*Notes from Blackfriars, Satyres and Satyricall Epigrams*).

Samuel Sheppard, on the other hand, singles out *The White Devil* for praise in his *Epigrams Theological, Philosophical and Romantic* (1651) calling it '*Mr Webster's Most Excellent Tragedy*'. It was revived after the Restoration in 1661 and again in 1671. Samuel Pepys saw it twice but thought it 'a very poor play' the first time (2 October 1661), recording in his diary two days later that it 'pleased me worse than it did the other day'. Interestingly the play was entitled *Vittoria Corombona*, suggesting a new-found prominence for the role in a theatre in which women, rather than boys, now took the female parts. Nahum Tate had adapted Shakespeare's *King Lear* in 1687 for the Restoration stage by simplifying the language and giving it a happy ending. In 1707 he reworked *The White Devil* eliminating its complexity, **ambiguity** and bawdiness. Significantly his version, *Injur'd Love, or the Cruel Husband, a Tragedy*, does not mention his source, suggesting that Tate did not expect Webster's work to be recognised as the original.

CRITICAL HISTORY

As with all playwrights of the early modern period, Webster has generally been seen in relation to and compared (unfavourably) with Shakespeare. Critical writing has centred on his two great tragedies, *The White Devil* and *The Duchess of Malfi*, which are often discussed together. Both plays have provoked controversy and disagreement, often described as decadent and **melodramatic**. Criticism has focused on the plays' sensational qualities, complicated plot structure and ambiguous morality.

Romantic critics were enthusiastic about Elizabethan and Jacobean drama and Webster was one of many playwrights retrieved by them from antiquarian obscurity. Charles Lamb wrote admiringly about *The White Devil*, picking out 'The Arraignment of Vittoria' (III.2), arguing that 'This White Devil of Italy sets off a bad cause so speciously, and pleads with such an innocence-resembling boldness, that we seem to see that matchless beauty of her face which inspires such gay confidence into her', as well as 'Cornelia's Dirge' (V.4) (*Specimens of the English Dramatic Poets Who Lived about the Time of Shakespeare*, 1808). In a series of lectures on Elizabethan drama William Hazlitt suggested that Webster was 'the nearest to Shakespear [sic] of any thing we have' and was equally enthusiastic about Vittoria, whom he saw as 'fair as the leprosy, dazzling as the lightening' (*Collected Works*, VI, pp. 240–1). No one was more fulsome in his praise than the poet Swinburne, who likened Webster to Aeschylus, proclaiming 'this great poet – a greater than all since Shakespeare – has expressed the latent mystery of terror which lurks in all the highest poetry or beauty' (A. C. Swinburne, 'Chance and Terror in Webster' from 'John Webster', *Nineteenth Century*, vol. 19, no. 112, 1886, pp. 868–9). The poet and scholar Rupert Brooke recognised the 'solidity and immensity of Webster's mind' and yet is finally repelled, 'A play of Webster's is full of the feverish and ghastly turmoil of a nest of maggots. Maggots are what the inhabitants of this universe most resemble … Human beings are writhing grubs in an immense night. And the night is without stars or moon' (*John Webster and the Elizabethan Drama*, 1916, pp. 136–58, reprinted in *John Webster: A Critical Anthology*, 1969, pp. 88–94, p. 94).

Charles Kingsley admitted that 'they are pretty generally agreed to be the best tragedies written since Shakespeare's time' but for him they were merely sensational: 'The whole story of *Vittoria Corombona* is one of sin and horror … the study of human nature is not Webster's aim. He has to arouse terror and pity, not thought' (*North British Review*, vol. 25, 1856). The drama critic William Archer (1826–1924) objected to revivals of the plays of Webster and his contemporaries on the grounds of their lack of realism and rational plot construction, dismissing a production of *The Duchess of Malfi* as 'three hours of coarse and sanguinary melodrama' (quoted in *John Webster: A Critical Anthology*, 1969, p. 51).

 CHECK THE BOOK

Charles Kingsley (1819–75) was an English scholar, cleric and novelist. He was an advocate of 'muscular Christianity' and espoused social reform in his best-known novel *The Water Babies* (1863), a fairytale about the life of a poor boy forced to work as a chimney sweep. He also wrote a historical romance called *Westward Ho!* set in the Elizabethan period and using the same name as one of Webster's plays.

CHECK THE NET

George Bernard Shaw (1856–1950) was one of the most important, influential, brilliant and distinguished writers of the twentieth century. He was a committed Fabian, that is a socialist intellectual, and his plays dealt with social issues in uncompromising and often disconcerting ways. He was also a distinguished and often hilarious music and drama critic. He was awarded the Nobel Prize for Literature in 1925 and you can find further details of his life at **http://nobelprize. org** – enter 'Shaw' into the search box and click on 'biography'.

George Bernard Shaw speaks of 'the opacity that prevented Webster … from appreciating his own stupidity' (*Our Theatre in the Nineties*, Constable, 1932, vol. III, p. 317).

Twentieth-century critics proved less squeamish and more appreciative than the Victorians. They recognised in the world invoked in Webster's uncompromising tragic vision the horrors and seemingly infinite possibilities for evil in their own experience of two World Wars. T. S. Eliot's seminal essay in *Four Elizabethan Dramatists* (1924, revised and republished as *Elizabethan Dramatists*, Faber, 1963) was hugely influential on critical appreciation of the non-naturalistic elements in early modern drama. Focus has been on genre – how the play relates to the morality tradition and revenge drama – for example in the work of distinguished English literary critics such as L. C. Knights or L. G. Salingar; and structure and morality – attempts to analyse, defend or critique Webster's organisation of his material – in the works of G. Wilson Knight (*The Wheel of Fire*, Oxford University Press, 1930), Una Ellis-Fermor (*The Jacobean Drama*, Methuen, 1936), Ian Jack (*Scrutiny*, 1949), Travis Bogard (*The Tragic Satire of John Webster*, Cambridge University Press, 1955).

More recently Ralph Berry has argued in *The Art of John Webster* (Clarendon Press, 1972) that Webster, often regarded as simply decadent, can be seen as part of the move from a classical to a romantic aesthetic in the development of the baroque, that is an art based on feeling rather than form: 'baroque art, more specifically, exhibits two main areas of interest: the depiction of extreme states of emotion, and the development of naturalism (as a concern of subject-matter and style). It is obsessively concerned with death and the flux of time' (p. 9). Jacqueline Pearson, in her book *Tragedy and tragicomedy in the plays of John Webster* (Manchester UP, 1980), looks at the whole of Webster's career, arguing for a perceived coherence throughout in the sustained combination of **tragedy** and **tragicomedy** in his plays.

CONTEMPORARY APPROACHES

Contemporary ideas about the play have been influenced by the development of literary theory in the 1980s and 1990s, drawing attention to the play's active engagement with its own historical moment – the early modern period – in terms of its politics of gender and class in Feminist and Marxist accounts. It has also been related to our own historical moment in post-modern accounts which draw attention to the play's **irony**, **ambiguity**, complexity and **metatheatricality**.

FEMINISM

Feminist criticism is centrally concerned with the role and representation of women in literature as producers, consumers and subjects. According to Catherine Belsey, it 'attends to the power relations inscribed in the areas patriarchal history treats as incidental: sexuality, private life and personal relations, cultural difference itself' (in her general editor's introduction to Valerie Traub's *Desire and Anxiety: Circulations of Sexuality in Shakespearean Drama*, Routledge, 1992, p. ix). The position of women in Webster's plays has long been recognised as a central concern and it is significant that his two great tragedies are focused on women – *The Duchess of Malfi* self-evidently – but the 'White Devil' of the title is most commonly taken to be Vittoria and for many years the play was known as *Vittoria Corombona*. Kate Aughterson, for example, simply states 'Webster's central characters are women' (*Webster: The Tragedies,* Palgrave, 2001, p. 83).

Gender is one of any society's most important categories for organising itself and the so-called 'woman question' (that is the debate over what it means to be a 'woman' and her appropriate place and role in society) was an important feature of early modern culture. Social anxieties about the changing nature of these societies and women's position within them became an important topic in other discourses as well as drama in the period. Much of the debate focuses on women's behaviour. Disquiet over masculine women was expressed and conduct books of the period lay down ideas for the feminine ideal. These include William Harrington, *Commendations of Matrimony* (1528); Heinrich Bullinger, *The Christen State of*

 CHECK THE BOOK

'Literary theory' is an umbrella term which covers many different approaches to literature. It has a long history going back to at least the *Poetics* of Aristotle but assumed increased importance in the second half of the twentieth century as new theoretical approaches were developed. There are many useful primers including Terry Eagleton's *Literary Theory: An Introduction* (1983) or Jonathan Culler's *Literary Theory: A Very Short Introduction* (1997).

FEMINISM continued

Matrimony (1541); William Whately, *A Bride-bush* (1617); Alexander Nowell, *Catechism* (1573); *Hic Mulier or the Man-Woman* (1620); William Gouge, *Of Domesticall Duties* (1622). The exact nature of the relation between ideal and actual and the extent to which women conformed to or rebelled against it, though, is hard to establish.

CHECK THE BOOK

Juliet Dusinberre's *Shakespeare and the Nature of Women* was one of the first feminist texts on Renaissance plays.

Feminist critics such as Juliet Dusinberre have argued that 'The drama from 1590 to 1625 is feminist in sympathy' (*Shakespeare and the Nature of Women*, Macmillan, 1975, p. 5). In their view, many of the plays examine critically the ways in which women are oppressed by, and respond to, social pressures, conforming to or resisting them. Vittoria is certainly central in *The White Devil* – it is her beauty and brilliance that inflame Brachiano's desire and thus activate the plot. A feminist critique might point out that her life is circumscribed entirely by her relations with men. She is unhappily married to an unsuitable mate, the object of Brachiano's desire, and employed as an instrument in her brother's determination to advance himself socially. Vittoria's life, in other words, seems to be defined by her place in a **patriarchal** social structure in which women are dependent upon and subservient to men.

CONTEXT

One of feminism's most trenchant criticisms of the representation of women in literature is that they have traditionally been assigned very limited subject positions – often seen as the 'virgin/whore' dichotomy, that is, they conform to limited stereotyped roles – either they are as good as gold or as wicked as sin.

Vittoria's ambition and the expression of her personal sexual desires are obstacles to the smooth working of such a system and, in the world of the play, have to be punished. Hence she is blamed and vilified by Monticelso as a 'whore' in the arraignment in Act III, and by Brachiano in Act IV, who is instantly ready to believe that she is unfaithful and does not hesitate to blame her and even sees himself as an innocent victim:

> Thou hast led me, like an heathen sacrifice,
> With music and with fatal yokes of flowers
> To my eternal ruin. Woman to man
> Is either a god or a wolf. (IV.2.87–90)

For the audience Vittoria's greatest triumph is in her arraignment when she confronts Monticelso fearlessly and defeats him in argument. However, she herself is well aware of her speaking out in public as a transgression of social codes and takes pains to apologise humbly to the Ambassadors: 'Humbly thus, / Thus low, to the most worthy and respected / Lieger ambassadors, my modesty / And womanhood I tender' (III.2.130–3). She goes on specifically to draw attention to the fact that in order to defend herself she 'Must personate masculine virtue to the point' (III.2.136). This scene and Vittoria's behaviour in it has, more than any other, engaged the attention of critics over the centuries demonstrating its importance and dramatic power in the conflicting interpretations it has evoked. In it Vittoria seems both brave and admirable at the same time as being a liar and a hypocrite.

In fact all the women in the play, despite their differences, are seen to be similarly positioned. Vittoria is specifically contrasted with the compliant, submissive Isabella, but her brother confirms that she was also subject to an arranged marriage with Brachiano in order to cement the alliance between Florence and Padua:

> Thou hast a wife, our sister; would I had given
> Both her white hands to death, bound and locked fast
> In her last winding-sheet, when I gave thee
> But one. (II.1.64–7)

Francisco now regrets giving her to Brachiano in marriage, wishing that she had died instead. In either case it suggests his conviction that Isabella was his to dispose of as he saw fit rather than as she chose. In order to preserve the peace Isabella play-acts a scene in which she furiously turns on her husband with the telling words: 'O that I were a man, or that I had power / To execute my apprehended wishes' (II.1.242–3). As soon as she does (even in pretence) vent her anger, she is immediately criticised and blamed: 'Now by my birth you are a foolish, mad / And jealous woman' (II.1.263–4).

Cornelia, too, is represented as a figure who has in Jonathan Dollimore's words, 'internalised her position as one of the exploited … By embracing the Christian ethic of humility and passive virtue' (*Radical Tragedy*, Harvester Wheatsheaf, 1984). As Dollimore points out, she **ironically** 'preaches to the Duke precisely the myth which ratifies his exploitation of subjects like her': 'The lives of princes should like dials move, / Whose regular example is so strong, / They make the times by them go right or wrong'

QUESTION

To what extent is the 'virgin/whore' dichotomy visible in the female characters of *The White Devil*?

CHECK THE BOOK

At I 2.200 Brachiano asks what the value is of Vittoria's 'jewel'. This was a term, like 'treasure' which was often used as a synonym for 'virginity' or 'maidenhead'. In a **patriarchal** society women's chief value was their power to continue the male line hence virginity was a priceless asset. As Ruth Kelso's *Doctrine for the Lady of the Renaissance* puts it, 'let a woman have chastity, she has all. Let her lack chastity and she has nothing' (p. 24).

(I.2.285–7). She curses her daughter and reproaches her son in her effort to uphold a status quo which is oppressing her. Brachiano however angrily asserts that she is the one responsible for all the ensuing trouble (I.2.303–5).

Zanche, Vittoria's Moorish maid, is oppressed by her race and class as well as gender, abused and insulted by Cornelia and Marcello and even by her lover, Flamineo. She is Vittoria's dark shadow, frequently referred to as 'devil', the black devil to Vittoria's white, and shares her mistress's fate.

One of the most disturbing elements in any feminist criticism must be the play's constant misogynistic commentary especially from Flamineo and Lodovico. Flamineo says, for example, 'women are like cursed dogs, civility keeps them tied all daytime, but they are let loose at midnight; then they do most good or most mischief' (I.2.196–9). In this speech Flamineo seems to recognise that women's position is like a dog's in that they are tied up in subjection to a master, but typically he goes on to imply that all they are interested in, and good for, is nightly (sexual) activities. The audience has to consider the context and reason for such diatribes as well as its own response. As Kathleen McLuskie suggests:

> Dramatised misogyny, and its mirror image, the adulation of women, was (and is) undoubtedly part of the ideological process which sustained patriarchal power. However, it was also a source of jokes and horror and the contradictory ways in which dramatic texts modulate its influence to sustain and humanise its impact reveal the process by which different forces within contemporary ideology can co-exist at one and the same time. (*Renaissance Dramatists Feminist Readings*, Harvester Wheatsheaf, 1989, pp. 228–9)

In other words, plays were one of the sites in which contemporary ideas about women were aired and explored and constituted, and one of the ways in which such ideas could be staged, reproduced, resisted and challenged. *The White Devil* focuses on the social roles of women and represents a brilliant but controversial woman at its centre, which has served over the centuries to polarise debate and attitudes to the play.

QUESTION

Post-colonialism is another form of literary criticism, which focuses on the effect on colonised countries or individuals of living under the imposition of a powerful, usually Western, influence. Does the presence of Zanche, and to a certain extent the disguising of Francisco as a Moor, raise post-colonial questions?

MARXISM

Marxism is a form of cultural analysis originating in the writings of Karl Marx, specifically concerned with the material conditions of people's lives. It examines the relationship between social class and power, money and the ownership of the means of production. It sees history in terms of a struggle between the social classes and in general supports the side of the oppressed proletariat. As Karl Marx said in *The Communist Manifesto*:

> The history of all hitherto existing society is the history of class struggles. Freeman and slave, patrician and plebeian, lord and serf, guild-master and journeyman — in a word, oppressor and oppressed, stood in constant opposition to one another, carried on an uninterrupted, now hidden, now open fight, a fight that each time ended either in a revolutionary re-constitution of society at large or in the common ruin of the contending classes. (quoted in David McLellan (ed), *Karl Marx: Selected Writings*, Oxford UP, 1977, p. 222)

A Marxist reading, therefore, will focus on the representation of the relations of power and class in a text. It will also examine the historical context of its production; an unsophisticated reading might attempt to read one off against the other, as though it offered an unproblematic representation of history. A Marxist analysis is especially useful in relation to *The White Devil* which is centrally concerned with the corruption and abuse of power in a feudal aristocracy, represented by the dukes of Brachiano and of Florence. The character who articulates the problem most clearly is Flamineo, who understands the system and that the only way to get on is by a willingness to carry out Brachiano's wishes, however illegitimate, 'Knaves do grow great by being great men's apes' (IV.2.243). As Dena Goldberg puts it:

> Flamineo ... is blocked by a discrepancy between his aspirations and the means available for their fulfilment. Raised and educated as a gentleman (in spite of the dwindling resources of his family), Flamineo is caught between upper class expectations and the realities of the job market. When we meet him he has long since

CHECK THE BOOK

Francis Wheen's excellent and very accessible biography *Karl Marx* was published by Fourth Estate in 1999.

CONTEXT

Feudalism is the term used by later historians to describe the social organisation of the middle ages, which was based on a system of reciprocal legal and military obligations between lords, vassals (one who holds lands from a lord) and fiefs (inherited estates in land held on condition of service to a superior lord).

CONTEXT

There was a great deal of contemporary anxiety around conspicuous consumption and the wasting of inheritance. Shakespeare's play *Timon of Athens* dramatises the profligate waste and feasting of undeserving hangers-on, as does Ben Jonson's *Volpone,* which considers the situation from the opposite perspective of how a clever con-man can make a fortune by stringing along the gullible.

learned that public service, for the talented but poor, means subservience to the caprices and corruptions of the great men who constitute the state. For all his brilliance and his energy and his Latin, he can never hope to achieve any greater dignity than what is accorded to the Duke of Brachiano's personal lackey. (*Between Worlds: A Study of the Plays of John Webster*, Wilfrid Laurier UP, 1987, p. 23)

Flamineo bitterly accuses his mother over their poverty, complaining 'Pray what means have you / to keep me from the galleys, or the gallows?' (I.2.313–4). Cornelia's response is attractive in its humility and seeming morality but impractical, as Goldberg points out, in view of the various statutes enacted in the period concerning the punishment of 'rogues and vagabonds': 'The average Jacobean could take little comfort in being poor but honest, for these laws made poverty and economic dislocation punishable offences, subject to imprisonment, whipping and deportation' (*Between Worlds*, 1987, p. 48).

Goldberg reads the play in terms of the conflict between a feudal aristocracy, based on the ownership of land and a subservient peasantry, and the values of a rising bourgeoisie, and points out that it was written a mere thirty years before the English Revolution and civil war (see *Between Worlds*, 1987, p. 3). This ambivalence is reflected in Flamineo's personal class position. At one level he seems like the representative of the rising bourgeoisie (the wealthy, self-made middle classes) and his criticisms echo the bourgeois criticism of the abuse of feudal power, but in fact, like Lodovico, he is a member of the decaying aristocracy and his attitude displays the same lax morality associated with the decaying class.

A Marxist reading, then, would see the fates of the various characters as socially determined, that is resulting specifically from their class and social position rather than an effect of Christian morality or the workings of a divine providence. The tragic events of the play are a result of an inequitable social system in which a few individuals are enabled access to power on the basis of an accident of birth, which they retain through the unscrupulous use of violence and the exploitation and oppression of the majority.

POSTMODERNISM

Postmodernism refers to a theoretical approach which focuses on surfaces, disjunctions, lack of coherence, playfulness, **irony** and elements of pastiche in art. Originally coined to critique Modernist architecture, with its rejection of traditional ideas and techniques, the term became more widely applied to other art forms. Cultural theorists used it to express the post-war sense of disillusion; Jean Baudrillard sees it as fundamentally the 'loss of the real' and the explosion of 'simulacra', that is simulated images, arguing that modern life has been overtaken by media representation. We might point to the explosion of 'reality TV' programmes, the popularity of *Big Brother*, 'Myspace' and 'Facebook' as contemporary examples. Jean-François Lyotard argues that the postmodern condition signifies Western society's loss of belief in the so-called 'grand narratives' of religion, history, science, Marxism and progress, and the Enlightenment project, modernism's 'emancipation of humanity', has failed (*The Post-modern Condition*, Manchester UP, 1988, p. 32).

Postmodern ideas often seem complicated and contradictory, but it is not difficult to see how such an approach might be applied to a play like *The White Devil* which is constantly drawing attention to its own fictional status: that it is really a play and should not be confused with 'real life'. This can be seen, for example, in the asides to the audience which break 'realistic' codes, to its use of **irony**, emphasis on playacting, and its self-conscious theatricality. A useful term in relation to such an analysis is **metadrama** or **metatheatre**, meaning 'above' or 'beyond' drama or theatre and is used to denote the ways in which plays specifically refer to their own theatricality, their status as play.

The presence of commentator-characters like Flamineo, constantly reminding the audience that they are watching a play, has the effect of distancing them from the characters and events. In Act I Scene 2, for example, at Camillo's approach, he informs the audience:

> See, here he comes; this fellow by his apparel
> Some men would call a politician,
> But call his wit in question, you shall find it
> Merely an ass in's foot-cloth. (I.2.48–51)

> **CONTEXT**
>
> Modernism is the term used to describe a cultural movement of the late nineteenth/early twentieth centuries which was committed to reforming traditional patterns of thinking, in ways which took account of modern industrial society's needs and aspirations. It questioned the nature of reality and led to abstract non-representational art forms. Modernist writers include Virginia Woolf, James Joyce, T. S. Eliot and Samuel Beckett.

CHECK THE NET

For more details on modernism in the visual arts go to: www.artsmia.org/modernism

Later when Flamineo and Lodovico meet, Marcello tells the audience 'Mark this strange encounter' (III.3.65). Flamineo's statement of his dramatic function, 'We are engaged to mischief and must on' (I.2.345) is clearly **metatheatrical**. His later greeting of Doctor Julio is completely over-the-top and seems designed to relish its own absurdity:

> O thou cursed antipathy to nature; look, his eye's bloodshed like a needle a chirurgeon stitcheth a wound with. Let me embrace thee toad, and love thee, [*Embraces him*] O thou abhominable loathsome gargarism, that will fetch up lungs, lights, heart, and liver by scruples. (II.1.306–11)

It is hard not to imagine that it would raise a laugh in the theatre as would the duke's deadpan, **ironic** response, 'No more; I must employ thee honest doctor' (II.1.312).

The use of devices such as the **dumb shows,** ghosts and masques again seem designed to highlight the play's theatricality and lack of realism, as does the constant recourse to the characters' play-acting – for example Isabella's public rejection of Brachiano. Despite the praise heaped on Vittoria's performance in court and what the critic Charles Lamb called her 'innocence-resembling boldness' the audience certainly recognise that at one level it is all a charade. Another strikingly modern element in the play is its mixture of tone and styles. Whereas traditional critics have felt uncomfortable with this and seen it as a failure on Webster's part, a postmodern reading would celebrate such aspects.

PART FIVE

BACKGROUND

JOHN WEBSTER'S LIFE AND WORKS

Little was known about Webster's life until 1976 when the scholar Mary Edmond published details of her research in the parish records of St Sepulchre-without-Newgate, the London parish in which Webster lived his entire life. His date of birth and death are still not certain – many records were lost in the Great Fire of London in 1666 – but we now know that Webster came from a prosperous family of London coach-makers. His father, also John Webster, was a member of one of the important livery companies, the Merchant Taylors, and a prosperous businessman. John Webster senior not only made coaches but hired out two-wheeled carts and four-wheeled wagons, as well as horses and all the necessary equipment, at a time when they were becoming fashionable. The business was located in the thriving commercial part of the city at the corner of Cow Lane and Hosier Lane, near Smithfield horse-market, next to the site of the annual Bartholomew Fair, vividly portrayed by Ben Jonson in his play of the same title. His customers ranged from the city authorities' civic pageants and the transporting of criminals to be hanged at Tyburn to the players' companies when they toured the country. One of the foremost Webster scholars has suggested that 'by the reign of King James, the elder Webster supervised a burgeoning establishment and was approaching the status of a Renaissance Henry Ford or Walter Chrysler' (Charles R. Forker, *Skull Beneath the Skin: The Achievement of John Webster*, Southern Illinois Press, 1986, p. 4).

John Webster was probably born around 1578–9. He had a younger brother, Edward, and several sisters. Since his father was a freeman of the Merchant Taylors Company, which was associated with coach-making – too new a business for a guild of its own – it is almost certain that he would have attended the Merchant Taylors School, one of the most famous in the country, which had been presided over for many years by the progressive educationalist Richard Mulcaster. There Webster would have acquired a grounding in Latin and the classics, studying grammar, logic, rhetoric,

QUESTION

Read Webster's address 'To the Reader' carefully. What are the main points Webster makes and how would you describe the tone of his address?

arithmetic, geometry, music and astronomy. There is no evidence of his attending university but a John Webster did enter the Middle Temple, one of the Inns of Court, in 1598 which scholars are generally agreed was most likely John Webster the playwright. The importance of the law in Webster's plays and his fondness for trial scenes would certainly suggest that he had some legal training, although this was a highly litigious age in which many people had acquaintance with the law. His younger brother Edward was apprenticed to his father and followed him into coach-making and it may be that the older son was intended to look after the legal and administrative side of the business. It is not clear how involved he actually was and whether he worked in the family business but if he did this would explain Henry Jeffrey's sneering jibe about 'crabbed Websterio … playwright cartwright' and might also explain why his output was rather slow.

Webster probably went straight from school to the New Inn (one of the minor Inns of Chancery) in 1596–7 and from there to the Middle Temple in 1598 where he could study not only the law but fencing, singing, dancing and other social accomplishments as well as theology, grammar, rhetoric, philosophy, poetry and logic. The Inns of Court were designed for the intellectually and socially privileged. Conveniently located between the city and the court at Westminster, they were something between a gentleman's finishing school and a university. The atmosphere was lively, competitive and intellectual; legal apprenticeship was mainly in the form of studying textbooks and trials and conducting arguments in law French. Not all those who attended took up the law and a number became writers including John Marston, John Ford, Francis Beaumont and Sir John Davies.

 CHECK THE NET

For an account of the life of Sir John Davies, Webster's contemporary at the Middle Temple, go to: **http://www. luminarium.org,** click on 'Renaissance' and then 'Sir John Davies'.

In 1605–6 at the age of twenty-six John Webster married Sara Penniall, daughter of Simon Penniall, a member of the Saddlers Company and a Warden of the City. They married in haste, during Lent, outside London since Sara was already seven months pregnant and their son, another John, was born two months later. Other children followed. In 1615, a year after his father's death, John Webster was himself made 'free' of the Merchant Taylors Company 'by patrimony', that is due to his father's position rather than 'by servitude' as his brother had been. Webster produced a steady flow of works – plays, pageants, and poems – until the mid 1630s. There is no record of Webster's death but in 1635 his old friend Thomas Heywood commends him along with other writers in his poem about writers' nicknames, *Hierarchie of the Blessed Angels,* in terms which suggest that he was no longer living:

> Fletcher and Webster, of that learned packe
> None of the mean'st, yet neither was but Iacke [Jack].

The first theatrical mention of Webster comes in Philip Henslowe's account book on 22 May 1602, when he is one of a group of writers to whom Henslowe 'lent' £5 in relation to a lost play called *Caesar's Fall*. The balance of £3 was paid a week later; although referred to as *Two Shapes* it is assumed to be the same play. Henslowe was a theatrical entrepreneur and owner of the Rose theatre. His meticulously kept accounts have proved an invaluable source of information for historical research. The other writers, with whom Webster was presumably collaborating, were Thomas Dekker, Michael Drayton, Thomas Middleton and Anthony Munday. It was the norm for plays to be written collaboratively and it would be usual for a young writer starting out to work with more experienced colleagues. Little is known about the play which presumably related the death of Julius Caesar, most likely to compete with Shakespeare's play of 1599 at the rival Globe theatre.

Six months later Webster is again collaborating with Dekker and others on a play dealing with more contemporary historical events, *Lady Jane* – referred to elsewhere as *The Overthrow of Rebels.* Another lost play, it concerned the tragic fate of the gentle, scholarly Lady Jane Grey whose ambitious family had claimed the English throne on her behalf. She reigned for nine days and was later beheaded by Mary I. The play was clearly a success since a second part was commissioned. It has been suggested that the surviving 'bad quarto' of a play called *Sir Thomas Wyatt* might be a garbled amalgamation of the two plays. Webster collaborated on another lost play, again with Dekker plus Henry Chettle and Thomas Heywood. This seems to have been a comedy called *Christmas Comes But Once a Year* presumably written for the festive season of 1602–3. He also wrote a short commendatory poem *'To my kinde friend …'* for the third part of Anthony Munday's translation of the Spanish romance *Palmerin of England.*

CHECK THE NET

For details of the Rose theatre of Webster's London go to: **www.britannia. com** and search for 'Rose theatre'.

CHECK THE BOOK

Andrew Gurr's *The Shakespearean Stage 1574–1642* (Cambridge University Press, 1992) gives a detailed account of theatrical practices in the period.

CONTEXT

Working with the King's Men would have given Webster the opportunity to meet the company's foremost actors such as Richard Burbage, Henry Condell, Hemings and Robert Armin as well as William Shakespeare.

In 1603 the theatres were closed due to one of the periodic outbreaks of the plague and the death of Queen Elizabeth I on 24 March. The following year Webster wrote 'Additions' for John Marston's **satirical tragicomedy** *The Malcontent* for the King's Men at the Globe, possibly with Marston himself, who had originally written it for the Children of Blackfriars Company. The influence of Marston's play can clearly be seen on Webster's later work, as Forker suggests that Marston 'managed not only to shift the emphasis of the older tradition by introducing the snarling satire and social moralising for which he was already notorious but also to increase the shock value by fusing 'camp' or absurdist humor, violence, horror, and sex against a background of Italianate decadence' (*Skull Beneath the Skin*, 1986, p. 75).

Webster worked with Dekker again on two more **comedies**, *Westward Ho* (1604) and *Northward Ho* (1605). These lively citizen comedies celebrate the uneasy mix of money, sex and honour. *Westward Ho*, the call of the Thames watermen plying their trade upriver, must have been a success since it inspired Jonson, Chapman and Marston to write *Eastward Ho*. The following year Dekker and Webster produced *Northward Ho*, concerning more illicit sexual encounters in the Hertfordshire town of Ware, north of London, and famous for its 'great bed'. Webster also contributed a commendatory ode to the *Arches of Triumph*, a volume of engravings and descriptions of the seven triumphal arches built to commemorate James I's entrance to London. It is possible that Webster also helped Dekker with writing the speeches for the occasion or with some of the descriptions, although if so his contribution is not recorded.

The next definite date for Webster's theatrical activity is the 1612 publication of *The White Devil*, his first solo-authored play which, we have seen, he admits took a long time to write and also that the first production was not a success. The play was based on recent historical events in Italy concerning Vittoria Accoromboni and the Duke de Brachiano (see **Historical background and sources**). It is not clear how long it took – the theatres were closed for long periods due to plague between 1605 and 1610. At the conclusion to *The White Devil*, instead of an epilogue, Webster wrote a short review which especially praised the acting of 'my friend Master

[Richard] Perkins' who had performed the role of Flamineo. In 1612 Thomas Heywood published his *Apology for Actors* which defended the theatre against the attack by puritans on moral grounds. Webster wrote a poem in warm support of the work. Shortly afterwards, in 1612, Henry, Prince of Wales, James I's popular eldest son, died unexpectedly and Webster wrote a three hundred and thirty line elegy entitled *A Monumental Column*, which he dedicated to Robert Carr, Viscount Rochester, James I's favourite courtier.

Webster's most popular and successful play, *The Duchess of Malfi*, was written and first performed some time in 1613–14 by the King's Men at the Blackfriars theatre, their smaller indoor venue used in winter. It was again based on scandalous recent events in Amalfi in Italy. The play was published in 1623 and the title page indicates that it was also performed at the Globe. This was the most prestigious acting company – Shakespeare was a shareholder (one of the founding members) and housekeeper – who played frequently at court, and signified a rise in Webster's reputation and recognition of his talents. The production was a success and was revived in 1619 with a new cast. It established Webster as a respected writer of **tragedies**.

In 1613 Webster's talented and widely admired friend Sir Thomas Overbury was poisoned by Frances Howard, then Countess of Essex, in a scandalous murder case, for his opposition to her marriage with his friend Robert Carr. Overbury had written a character sketch called *A Wife* which set out what every young man should seek in his marriage partner. It was widely believed he had written it as a warning to Carr and that Frances Howard was so incensed she planned Overbury's murder by slow poisoning. When foul play was later suspected, Frances Howard pleaded guilty although Robert Carr, now her husband, did not. Both were found guilty but later pardoned, but four of her accomplices were hanged. The sketch published posthumously in 1614 was a success and a second edition was brought out later in the year with additional sketches by Overbury and others. Webster contributed six of these including *An Excellent Actor*. Over the following years, in later editions, he added other characters including *A Fair and Happy Milkmaid* and *A True Character of a Dunce*. Overbury's

 CHECK THE NET

Visit the website of the reconstructed Shakespeare's Globe (the theatre opened in 1997), and their virtual tour of the building – go to **www.shakespeares-globe.org** and search for virtual tour.

CHECK THE NET
You can find details of the life of Richard Burbage and other relevant theatrical characters and practices at: **www.theatre database.com** – click on '16th Century theatre'.

Characters, as they are known, offer short, pithy thumbnail sketches of figures from contemporary life. Many set out to be witty and satirical but not all are hostile. Webster's portrait of *An Excellent Actor* is full of sincere warmth – it has been suggested that Richard Burbage, the leading actor with the King's Men, was his model:

> Whatsoever is commendable in the grave Orator, is most exquisitely perfect in him; for by a full and significant action of body, he charmes our attention ... Hee adds grace to the Poets labours: for what in the Poet is but ditty, in him is both ditty and musicke ... I observe of all men living, a worthy Actor in one kind is the strongest motive of affection that can be: for when he dies, we cannot be perswaded any man can doe his parts like him.

Webster was at the height of his dramatic powers and his next play, unfortunately lost, was a **tragedy** called *Guise* to which he refers in the later dedication of *The Devil's Lawcase*. It was probably written around 1615. The play dealt with the life and death by assassination of the colourful French Duke de Guise. Christopher Marlowe's play *The Massacre at Paris* featured Guise as an archetypal Machiavellian schemer. It is easy to see how the material would have appealed to Webster as a dramatic subject. Webster's next play *The Devil's Lawcase*, written between 1617–19, was a **tragicomedy** also influenced by one of Marlowe's plays, *The Jew of Malta*. It was put on at either the Red Bull or the Cockpit theatre (sometimes known as the Phoenix from the way it rose from the ashes of the earlier Cockpit) and published in 1623, the same year as Shakespeare's First Folio, the posthumous collection of his plays brought out by his theatrical colleagues Hemings and Condell.

Webster's final plays were again collaborations. It is thought that he may possibly have had a hand in Rowley, Dekker and Ford's domestic tragedy *The Witch of Edmonton* (1621), the year in which he wrote the city comedy *Anything for a Quiet Life* with Thomas Middleton. In 1623 Webster wrote eight lines of commendatory verse for Henry Cockeram's *English Dictionarie*. The next year he again collaborated with Dekker, Rowley and Ford in a bizarre drama which amalgamated two recent London scandals in a play called *A Late Murther of the Son upon the Mother, or Keep the*

Widow Waking (1624). In 1624 Webster was in charge of the pageant put on by the Merchant Taylors to celebrate the inauguration of one of their own company, Sir John Gore, as Lord Mayor of London on 29 October. Webster, as a freeman of the Company himself, must have seemed the obvious choice to produce the event. The Merchant Taylors spent £1,000 – an exorbitant sum for the time. Webster published his work almost immediately as *Monuments of Honor*. It featured the symbolic glorification of London and a number of characters representing learning including Chaucer, Gower, Lydgate, Sir Thomas More and Sir Philip Sidney, as well as heroes of the Merchant Taylors Company. Established as a public poet Webster was commissioned to compose celebratory verses for a portrait of the royal family.

Round about 1625 he wrote *A Cure for a Cuckold* with William Rowley who died in 1626, although the play was not published until 1661. Most scholars believe that Webster had a hand in *The Fair Maid of the Inn*, a play attributed to John Fletcher, who succeeded Shakespeare as playwright for the King's Men. The date of Webster's tragedy *Appius and Virginia* is uncertain. It may have been written earlier but most scholars think it was written after 1623 and marks a return on Webster's part to classical history for source material. Evidence suggests that Thomas Heywood may have contributed in part. The story relates the tale of a corrupt Roman magistrate and a father's sacrifice of his daughter in order to save her honour. Chaucer used the same story as his *Physician's Tale* in *The Canterbury Tales*, but Webster went back to Books X and XI of *Roman Antiquities* by Dionysius of Halicarnassus for the story. Webster's reputation today is based on his tragedies *The White Devil* and *The Duchess of Malfi*, together with the tragicomedy *The Devil's Lawcase*.

LITERARY BACKGROUND

WEBSTER'S THEATRE

Webster was writing at a time of cultural change and activity which offered great scope and opportunities for talented young men. The early modern period was characterised by developing use of the vernacular, increasing secularism in conjunction with the religious

> **CONTEXT**
> Collaborative writing was the norm, with over fifty per cent of plays in the period written by more than one playwright. It provided a practical solution to the acting companies' constant demand for new material and allowed young writers to work with experienced playwrights.

WEBSTER'S THEATRE continued

CHECK THE BOOK

Steven Mullaney's *The Place of the Stage: License, Play and Power in Renaissance England* (University of Chicago Press, 1995) discusses the ambiguous social and intellectual situation of the drama at this period.

CHECK THE NET

Go to: **http://www. william-shakespeare. info/elizabethan- theatre-locations. htm** for a map of the location of the London theatres. From this you can see that the majority are located outside the city and thus outside the control of the city authorities.

Reformation, the collapse of feudalism, the development of trade, merchant capitalism, increasing education and literacy, social mobility, and a movement to the towns. At the same time more indefinable influences of the Reformation and Renaissance humanism led to new ways in which individuals thought about themselves and their place in the world. These factors combined to influence the development of a secular drama against hostility from the Church and civil authorities. There were numerous anti-theatrical and anti-poetic treatises and pamphlets published in the period, such as John Northbrooke's *Treatise Against Dicing, Dancing, Plays and Interludes with Other Idle Pastimes* (1577), Stephen Gosson's *School of Abuse* (1579), Philip Stubbes's *Anatomy of Abuses* (1579), and *A Second and Third Blast of Retrait from Plaies and Theaters* (1580). Despite these the theatre became enormously popular as a form of entertainment and the repertory system of the acting companies required a constant supply of new material from the numbers of young men from the universities, the Inns of Court and, in some cases such as Shakespeare, actors turned writer. Most plays were written collaboratively, sometimes with as many as five or six writers. The drama of the Elizabethan and early Jacobean period is now regarded as one of the highpoints of English literature, as it produced William Shakespeare, Ben Jonson, Christopher Marlowe, Francis Beaumont, John Fletcher and Thomas Middleton among the names of illustrious writers who produced comedies, tragedies, histories, pastoral plays and tragicomedies to order.

At the beginning of the sixteenth century there were various playing spaces available for staging a dramatic performance. There were public spaces such as inns or courtyards in which itinerant companies of strolling players, tumblers and jugglers who travelled the country, played in makeshift locations, mainly in the larger towns. Plays were also performed in private houses and halls, the universities – only Oxford and Cambridge at this time – or the Inns of Court. It was not until 1576 that the first permanent theatre was erected in Shoreditch by James Burbage, a craftsman joiner and father of Richard. The theatres were located outside the city walls, in the suburbs and outside the jurisdiction of the city fathers and their continued opposition. Those inside the city were within what were known as 'liberties' – technically a district within a city but not subject to the city authorities such as Blackfriars or the Clink. Companies were adaptable and used to playing in whatever spaces were available in inn-yards and halls. When they came to build permanent theatres or playhouses, the basic design was inspired by the classical amphitheatre but the specific design varied from theatre to theatre. The earliest amphitheatres, such as the Red Lion in Stepney, consisted of a raised platform backed by a curtained booth for the players with a yard and banks of scaffolding supporting benches for the audience around the stage. Later designs were more sophisticated, either round, polygonal – the Globe (1599) Shakespeare's 'wooden O' was in fact polygonal – or square like the Fortune. They consisted of an apron stage, up to forty feet across, which thrust forward into the yard and was supported by two pillars with a painted ceiling (the heavens) over it which provided shelter for the actors. It could be used for technical apparatus as in descents and flying. There was a tiring-house to the rear which functioned as a dressing-room for the actors with a gallery above, which could be used as additional playing-space. The front of the tiring-house had a number of openings from where actors made their entrances. Some theatres had a large trap door near the front of the stage. The décor of the theatres was rich and colourful with carved and painted wood and beautiful hangings. These were draped in black for tragedies.

There were a number of differences between the Elizabethan and Jacobean outdoor theatres and modern theatres. Plays were performed in daylight and audiences were required to participate actively in the imaginative experience – this also meant that audience members could see each other and interact amongst themselves. Theatres could hold up to three thousand spectators necessitating 'dramatic' speech and a large gestural acting style. Because of the apron stage, the audience was also very close – in some cases, such as the Red Bull, members of the audience were allowed to sit on the edge of the stage for an extra payment. These conditions favoured dramatic techniques such as **soliloquies**, **asides** and direct audience address to draw in the crowd. Self-reflexive techniques were also common, drawing attention to the play as performance. The lack of props and sets further enhanced the stylisation and ritualistic quality of the action. Another important difference was that women's parts were played by boys or young men as it was thought unsuitable for women to appear on stage.

 CHECK THE BOOK

In the Prologue to *Henry V* Shakespeare draws attention to the inadequacies of the theatre to represent huge battle scenes and requests the aid of the audience's imagination to aid the attempt: 'Can this cockpit hold / The vasty fields of France? Or may we cram / Within this wooden O, the very casques / That did affright the air at Agincourt?'

WEBSTER'S THEATRE continued

CONTEXT

Sir John Davies reflected the diversity of theatre audiences in a contemporary epigram (?1593): 'For as we see at all the playhouse doors,/ When ended is the play, the dance, and song,/ A thousand townsmen, gentlemen, and whores,/ Porters and serving-men together throng'.

Audiences covered a fairly wide social spectrum at the public theatres – private theatres were more select and more expensive. There was considerable critical comment about audiences – that they were noisy, badly-behaved and unappreciative as Webster suggests in *The White Devil*'s address 'To the Reader'. Despite the increasing use of more expensive indoor theatres over the period, the playhouses were enormously popular and attracted a socially mixed audience.

SENECA AND THE TRAGEDY OF BLOOD

Seneca was an important influence on the development of Renaissance drama. His **tragedies** inspired Elizabethan writers in terms of structure, tone and subject matter. Lucius Annaeus Seneca was born in Spain in 4 BC but had been educated in Rome and became famous not only as a playwright but as an orator and philosopher. He had been tutor to the young Emperor Nero and later became his advisor. It was after Seneca retired in AD 62 that Nero accused him of conspiracy and he was forced to commit suicide. It's not clear whether Seneca's plays were written for public performance or whether they were intended for recitation before a small private audience. Traditionally ten tragedies were ascribed to him, all adaptations from earlier, mainly Greek, sources. Eight of these are now considered authentic: *Oedipus* from Sophocles's *Oedipus Tyrannos*, *Agamemnon* from Aeschylus's play, *Thyestes* from an unknown source (probably a Latin play), and the rest from Euripides. They are characterised by scenes of violence, mutilation and horror, and also display a fascination with magic, death and the supernatural. They are structured in five episodes, separated by choral interludes, with use of **soliloquies** and **asides** and littered with moral *sententiae* (moral maxims), all of which became characteristic of Renaissance drama. The plays became popular reading in the sixteenth century and were widely available in Latin. They were subsequently translated into English by John Studley in 1566 and by Thomas Marsh in 1581. Thomas Kyd, also a pupil of the Merchant Taylors' School, is the first playwright generally credited with popularising tragedies inspired by Seneca in *The Spanish Tragedy*, written in the late 1580s. He is thought to have written an early version of *Hamlet* which Shakespeare subsequently rewrote. It is not difficult to see how Webster was influenced by Senecan dramaturgy especially in his tragedies, *The White Devil* and *The Duchess of Malfi*, with their scenes of sensational violence and horror, their preoccupation with death and the supernatural, together with their witty commentary by **malcontents** such as Flamineo and Bosola (the parallel character in *The Duchess*), and their use of *sententiae (see* **Language: Style and tone***)*.

THE GOTHIC TRADITION

It will be obvious from the foregoing discussion that in stylistic terms, **gothic** has quite a lot in common with the description of Senecan drama. Originally gothic referred to the Germanic tribes who conquered Rome (the Ostrogoths and Visigoths) but used as a cultural term it came to stand for anti-classical, that is the opposite to the balanced, rational compositions of classical art and architecture associated with Roman civilization. It was used pejoratively to mean rude and barbaric in design. As a contemporary youth sub-culture often gothic describes an intellectualised anti-establishment attitude, with an eccentric style of dress and hair, usually all in black.

In literary terms gothic describes an emphasis on feeling and sensation over ideas and reason. It was associated with anti-Catholic sentiment, the critique of Roman Catholic excesses, and inspired by all things medieval. This is opposed to the Renaissance interest in the classical world which led to neoclassicism, to the Enlightenment and the Age of Reason. Gothic was used to describe the late eighteenth-century sensationalist fiction of Horace Walpole's *The Castle of Otranto* (1764) and Ann Radcliffe's *The Mysteries of Udolpho* (1794). The most extreme example is probably Matthew Lewis's *The Monk* (1796). It became associated with Romantic reaction to neoclassicism in its emphasis on feeling and was treated with some disdain by serious critics. Some Romantic poets dabbled in gothic effects in poems such as Keats's *The Eve of St Agnes* or Coleridge's *Christabel.* Jane Austen's *Northanger Abbey* is a **satire** on the gothic novel. Today it is often accompanied by the word 'horror' and applied to classic lurid tales of the supernatural, such as Bram Stoker's *Dracula* or Edgar Allen Poe's *The Fall of the House of Usher.* Many well-known Victorian works contain gothic

 CHECK THE BOOK
Ann Radcliffe's *The Mysteries of Udolpho* (1794) is an approachable and typical example of gothic literature, set in Italy like *The White Devil*. For more on the importance of setting, see **Historical background: London, Venice and Rome.**

THE GOTHIC TRADITION continued

elements such as Emily Brontë's *Wuthering Heights,* Charlotte Brontë's *Jane Eyre* or Charles Dickens's *The Mystery of Edwin Drood*. Twentieth-century examples include Daphne du Maurier's *Rebecca* or Susan Hill's *The Woman in Black*. From the beginning the genre often demonstrated a knowing, tongue-in-cheek self-awareness and tendency to self-**parody**. The best-known modern versions of gothic are probably the TV horror spoof *The Addams Family,* or *Buffy the Vampire Slayer*.

HISTORICAL BACKGROUND AND SOURCES

VITTORIA ACCOROMBONI

CHECK THE BOOK

Gabrielle Langdon's *Medici Women: Portrait of Power, Love and Betrayal from the Court of Duke Cosimo I* (Toronto UP, 2006), contains an Epilogue on Vittoria Accoromboni, and portraits of other women of her class. You can find a copy of the book online.

For the subject of his famous **tragedies** Webster selected two recent aristocratic Italian sex scandals. *The White Devil* is based on the history of Vittoria Accoromboni although Webster's play deviates significantly from the numerous accounts of the story which were published. Vittoria was born in 1557 at Gubbio (not Venice as Monticelso claims), a small town in Tuscany. Her family was aristocratic but poor and moved to Rome to improve their fortunes. Vittoria was a great beauty, full of charm and gaiety and, despite her modest dowry, she married Francesco Peretti, nephew to the powerful Cardinal Montalto in Rome, when she was only sixteen. About seven years later she met Paulo Giordano Orsini, Duke of Bracciano and became his lover, partly through the determined efforts of her ambitious mother and her scheming brother Marcello, who was in his service. The duke was twenty years older than her, physically obese and already married to Isabella de Medici, sister of the Grand Duke of Tuscany, and was the father of her three children. Isabella, however, was having an affair with a relative of her husband's, Troilo Orsini. Not all accounts agree on responsibility for the events which followed but it seems that Isabella's brother arranged for the death of her lover, Troilo Orsini, and either her brother or her husband (or the two together) arranged for Isabella to meet her own death. Marcello meanwhile shot Peretti in a deserted alley leaving Bracciano and Vittoria free to marry.

The then Pope Gregory XIII ordered the couple to separate and while an inquiry into Peretti's death was held, Vittoria was imprisoned in the Castello San Angelo in Rome. The investigations revealed nothing, however, and Vittoria was released. She and Bracciano married for a second time and lived together on his ancestral estates. The Pope continued his disapproval of the union and when he died four years later they celebrated with a third wedding in public, only to learn that Cardinal Montalto had been elected as the new pope, now Sixtus V. They fled from Bracciano, part of the Papal States, and went to Venice and Padua. The duke, however, was seriously ill; he suffered from a leg ulcer as well as his excessive corpulence and he died by Lake Garda in November 1585. Vittoria attempted suicide but failed and she returned to Padua but Isabella's family saw her as a threat to Isabella's son, Virginio's, inheritance. They hired Lodovico Orsini, a banished kinsman of the duke, to kill Vittoria and her younger brother Flaminio. Lodovico was later captured and strangled and his accomplices publicly executed. The Duke of Florence died two years later, most likely from poison and Marcello was extradited to Ancona where he was beheaded, while the Greek sorceress he had employed to give Bracciano aphrodisiacs was burned alive. Webster recognised the possibilities in these sensational events to enable him to fashion his own dark, intense tragedy.

LONDON, VENICE AND ROME

The Italy of English playwrights from the 1580s on was not a geographer's record but a fantasy setting for dramas of passion, Machiavellian politics, and revenge – a landscape of the mind (Ann Rosalind Jones, 'Italians and Others: *The White Devil* [1612]' in *Staging the Renaissance*, Routledge, 1991, p. 251).

John Webster, then, was by no means the only playwright to set plays in Italy – Shakespeare does in *The Two Gentlemen of Verona*, *The Taming of the Shrew*, *The Merchant of Venice* and *Romeo and Juliet* among others; Ben Jonson's *Volpone* is also set there, as is Thomas Middleton's *Women Beware Women* and John Ford's *'Tis Pity She's a Whore*. The northern spread of the Renaissance saw the introduction of Italian influence on ideas and in the arts, on fashions, poetry and manners. In the public imagination, Italy represented everything gorgeous, exotic, romantic, wicked and corrupt. Roger Ascham describes how its reputation had fallen in *The Scholemaster* (1570):

 CHECK THE BOOK

The Rialto in Venice was well-known to the playgoing public in Webster's day from its importance as a **symbolic** location in Shakespeare's play *The Merchant of Venice*, representing the commercial heart of the city where Shylock makes his bond with Antonio for a 'pound of flesh'.

Virtue once made that country Mistress over all the world. Vice now maketh that country slave to them that before were glad to serve it. All men seeth it: they themselves confess it, namely such as be best and wisest amongst them. For sin, by lust and vanity, hath and doth breed up everywhere, common contempt of God's word, private contention in many families, open factions in every City: and so, making themselves bound, to vanity and vice at home, they are content to bear the yoke of serving strangers abroad. *Italy* now is not that *Italy* that it was wont to be: and therefore now not so fit a place as some do count it for young men to fetch either wisdom or honesty from thence.

Italy was associated with the refined aristocratic manners described in Baldassare Castiglione's influential *Il Cortegiano* (1528), translated into English by Sir Thomas Hoby as *The Book of the Courtier* (1561) or with Petrarch's *Sonnets* on the one hand, and with Niccolò Machiavelli's analysis of the ruthless realpolitik of Renaissance princes, *The Prince*, on the other. In post-Reformation England it was especially associated with Roman Catholicism and the Pope in Rome. Lurid tales of sexual scandal, political corruption, passion, jealousy and revenge set in Italy were a favourite literary theme. As Isabella says in *The White Devil* 'my jealousy, / I am to learn what that Italian means' (II.1.160–1).

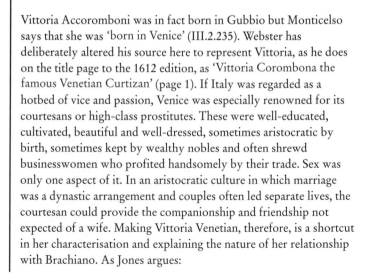

CHECK THE NET

For a virtual tour of Renaissance Venice go to: **www. italyguides.it** and click on 'Venice'.

Vittoria Accoromboni was in fact born in Gubbio but Monticelso says that she was 'born in Venice' (III.2.235). Webster has deliberately altered his source here to represent Vittoria, as he does on the title page to the 1612 edition, as 'Vittoria Corombona the famous Venetian Curtizan' (page 1). If Italy was regarded as a hotbed of vice and passion, Venice was especially renowned for its courtesans or high-class prostitutes. These were well-educated, cultivated, beautiful and well-dressed, sometimes aristocratic by birth, sometimes kept by wealthy nobles and often shrewd businesswomen who profited handsomely by their trade. Sex was only one aspect of it. In an aristocratic culture in which marriage was a dynastic arrangement and couples often led separate lives, the courtesan could provide the companionship and friendship not expected of a wife. Making Vittoria Venetian, therefore, is a shortcut in her characterisation and explaining the nature of her relationship with Brachiano. As Jones argues:

… if Vittoria comes across as 'less' (or indeed more) than 'a natural woman' it is because as a literary construction she distills English fantasies of Italianate excesses into an unstable personification of Venetian vice and allure ('Italians and Others', 1991, p. 256).

One of the most popular dramatic genres on the Jacobean stage was city **comedy**, set in London and dealing with topical contemporary events. However as Jonson, Marston and Chapman found with *Eastward Ho* (1605), their response to Webster and Dekker's *Westward Ho* (1604), even comedy could be dangerous, as Jonson and Chapman were arrested and imprisoned and Jonson threatened with having his ears and nose slit for anti-Scottish remarks in the play. Many writers then felt that social **satire** and criticism was often safer set at some distance, Italy being a convenient distance and a conventional location. Although *The White Devil* is set in Rome and is ostensibly concerned with events in Italy, it clearly glances at the court of James I which was notoriously corrupt with a reputation for loose sexual morals. The most notorious example is the scandalous affair of Frances Howard, Countess of Essex, with the king's favourite, Robert Carr, the annulment of her marriage, her subsequent marriage to Carr and poisoning of Webster's friend Thomas Overbury, who had warned against the marriage.

The play contains numerous references to Jacobean London such as Flamineo's accusatory question to Vittoria and Zanche after they have at shot him: 'How cunning you were to discharge! Do you practise at the Artillery Yard?' (V.6.157–8) referring to the weekly exercises for merchants and citizens in the Artillery Gardens at Bishopsgate. Dena Goldberg argues that one of the main themes the play explores is the inadequacy of the law for dealing with contemporary life since its structure 'reflects the structure of power in the society' and is fundamentally corrupt. In arguing that the play has much to do with English crime and law, Goldberg refers readers to 'Monticelso's black book, which contains a catalogue of crime that must appear conspicuously English to anyone who is familiar with the pamphlet literature of the period. Even Francisco's meditation on the black book is just an echo of popular satire on the extortion practised by minor court officials (IV.1.47–91)' (*Between Worlds: A Study of the Plays of John Webster* (Southern Illinois UP, 1986, p. 49).

 CHECK THE BOOK

Goldberg emphasises throughout her book the numerous parallels between the worlds of *The White Devil* and Jacobean London.

Historical Background	Webster's Life and Works	Literary Background
	1579/80 birth of John Webster	
1586 Richard Mulcaster leaves Merchant Taylors School; Trial of Mary Queen of Scots		**1586** Death of Sir Philip Sidney; Birth of John Ford
1587 Execution of Mary Queen of Scots	**1587?** Webster enters Merchant Taylors School	**1587** Rose Theatre opens
1588 Defeat of Spanish Armada		
	1589 Sara Peniall baptised 20 April	
1590s High prices leading to economic depression especially in countryside		**1590** Sidney's *Arcadia* published; Boys' Theatres (attached to schools such at St Paul's) were closed; Shakespeare, *Comedy of Errors, Henry VI Part 1*
		1591 Shakespeare, *Henry VI Part 2;* Anon, *Arden of Faversham*
1592 Plague: theatres close for two years		**1592** Marlowe, *Dr Faustus;* Shakespeare, *Henry VI Part 3*
		1593 Marlowe dies; Shakespeare, *Richard III, Two Gentlemen of Verona*
1594 Period of bad harvests begins		**1594** Shakespeare, *Love's Labour's Lost, The Taming of the Shrew*

Historical Background	Webster's Life and Works	Literary Background
1595 Sir Walter Ralegh's voyage to Guiana; death of Sir Francis Drake and John Hawkins	**1595?** Webster enters New Inn	**1595** Shakespeare, *A Midsummer Night's Dream, Richard II, Romeo and Juliet*
		1596 Shakespeare, *King John, Merchant of Venice*
1597 English campaign in Low Countries	**1597** Webster admitted to the Middle Temple	**1597** Shakespeare, *Henry IV Part I*
1598 Poor Law established; John Davies expelled from Middle Temple		**1598** Stow's Survey *of London* published
1599 Earl of Essex fails to defeat rebels in Ireland		**1599** Globe theatre built; bishops order burning of satires; James VI of Scotland publishes *Basilikon Doron;* death of Edmund Spenser; Paul's theatre reopens; Dekker, *Shoemakers' Holiday;* Shakespeare, *Henry V, Julius Caesar, Much Ado About Nothing*
1600 East India Company chartered		**1600** Blackfriars theatre reopened; Fortune Theatre built; Kempe, *Nine Days' Wonder,* Marston; *Antonio and Mellida, Antonio's Revenge;* Shakespeare, *As You Like It, Merry Wives of Windsor, Twelfth Night*

Historical Background	Webster's Life and Works	Literary Background
1601 Revolt and execution of Essex; Duke of Bracciano visits London		**1601** Dekker, *Satiromastix;* Jonson *Poetaster;* Shakespeare, *Hamlet*
1602 Bodleian library founded	**1602** Webster writes *Caesar's Fall* or *Two Shapes* (lost) with Munday, Drayton, Middleton (May); *Lady Jane* with Chettle, Dekker, Heywood, Smith (Oct); *Christmas Comes but Once a Year* (lost) with Chettle, Dekker, Heywood	**1602** Shakespeare, *Troilus and Cressida*
1603 Elizabeth I dies; Accession of James I; Theatre companies under royal patronage	**1603** Webster writes Introduction to Marston's *The Malcontent*	**1603** Shakespeare, *Othello* Jonson, *Sejanus;* Dekker, *Wonderful Year;* Florio translation of Montaigne's *Essays*
1604 Coronation of James I; peace with Spain; Hampton Court Conference	**1604** Webster writes verses for Harrison's *Arches of Triumph;* Webster writes *Westward Ho* with Dekker	**1604** Shakespeare, *Measure for Measure*
1605 Gunpowder Plot foiled	**1605** Webster marries Sara Peniall; Webster writes *Northwood Ho*	**1605** Chapman, Jonson & Marston are imprisoned for *Eastwood Ho;* Shakespeare, *King Lear*
	1606 Webster's son John baptised	**1606** Middleton, *The Revenger's Tragedy;* Jonson, *Volpone;* Shakespeare, *Macbeth*

Historical Background	Webster's Life and Works	Literary Background
1607 Settlement of Virginia	**1607** *Sir Thomas Wyatt, Westward Ho, Northward Ho* published	**1607** Beaumont, *Knight of the Burning Pestle;* Shakespeare, *Antony and Cleopatra*
1608 King's Men take over Blackfriars Theatre		**1608** Milton born; Shakespeare, *Timon of Athens*
		1609 Shakespeare, *Coriolanus, Pericles* (with George Wilkins), *Sonnets*
1610 Galileo's work on telescopes published		**1610** Beaumont & Fletcher, *King and No King, Maid's Tragedy;* Jonson, *The Alchemist;* Shakespeare, *Cymbeline*
1611 Sir John Swinnerton, Merchant Taylor, Lord Mayor of London		**1611–12** *King James Bible* published; Shakespeare, *Winter's Tale, The Tempest;* Tourneur, *Atheist's Tragedy*
1612 Death of Henry Prince of Wales, heir to the throne	**1612** Webster's *The White Devil* performed at Red Bull theatre and published; Webster's brother, Edward, admitted to Merchant Taylors Company (by serving his apprenticeship)	**1612** Overbury's *Characters* 1st edition; Heywood, *Apology for Actors;* Shakespeare, *Henry VIII;* Bacon, *Essays*
1613 Marriage of Princess Elizabeth to the Elector Palatine; death of Thomas Overbury	**1613** Webster's *A Monumental Column* published; *The Duchess of Malfi* performed by King's Men at Blackfriars theatre; bequests made to Webster, his wife and children by a neighbour	**1613** Globe Theatre burned; Middleton, *A Chaste Maid in Cheapside*

Historical Background	Webster's Life and Works	Literary Background
	1614 death of Webster's father	**1614** Second Globe built; Hope theatre opens; Jonson, *Bartholomew Fair;* Ralegh, *History of the World* published
	1615 Webster admitted to Merchant Taylors Company (by patrimony); Webster edits 3rd edition of Overbury's *Characters*	
1616 William Harvey discovers the circulation of the blood; Earl and Countess of Somerset (Frances Howard) tried for murder of Thomas Overbury		**1616** Deaths of Shakespeare and Francis Beaumont; Jonson, *First Folio;* James I, *Works* published
	1617 *The Devil's Law Case* acted; Henry Fitzjeffrey's attack on 'Crabbed Websterio' in *Satyres*	**1617** Cockpit Theatre opens; damaged by riot reopens June
1618 Thirty Years War begins; Sir Walter Ralegh executed; Jonson walks to Scotland	**1618–23** *The Duchess of Malfi* acted with new cast	**1618** Stow *Summary of English Chronicles* published
1620 Pilgrims settle at Plymouth, Massachusetts		
1621 Francis Bacon impeached	**1621** Edward Webster marries Susan Walker	**1621** Middleton, *Women Beware Women;* Robert Burton publishes *The Anatomy of Melancholy*
	1622? Webster's *Appius and Virginia* acted by a company of Boys actors	**1622** Middleton & Rowley *Changeling*

Historical Background	Webster's Life and Works	Literary Background
1623 Prince Charles and Duke of Buckingham travel to Spain	**1623** *The Duchess of Malfi* published	**1623** Shakespeare's *First Folio* published
1624 War with Spain; Sir John Gore, Merchant Taylor, Lord Mayor, 1624–5	**1624** *A Late Murder of the Son Upon the Mother, Or Keep the Widow Waking* (lost) written by Webster, Ford, Dekker, Rowley; *Monuments Of Honour* performed and published; Webster writes *A Cure for a Cuckold* with Rowley, acted possibly by the King's Men since Rowley was a member of the company at that time	**1624** Middleton, *Game at Chess*; Donne, *Devotions*
1625 Death of James I; succession of Charles I; Charles marries Henrietta Maria of France	**1625** Webster collaborates with Ford & Massinger on Fletcher's *The Fair Maid of the Inn*; verses by Webster on engraving of Royal family **?1625–34** *Appius and Virginia*	**1625** Deaths of Fletcher, and John Florio; theatres close for plague
1627 Duke of Buckingham assassinated **1629** Parliament dissolved **1631** Queen Henrietta Maria acts in court masques	**1631** Second edition of *The White Devil* **1634** Heywood speaks of Webster in past tense in *The Hierarchy of the Blessed Angels*	**1626** Deaths of William Rowley, Francis Bacon **1627** Death of Middleton

WORKS OF JOHN WEBSTER

Donald Beecher (ed.), *Overbury's Characters*, Dovehouse editions, 2003

Elizabeth M. Brennan (ed.), *The Devils' Lawcase*, New Mermaids, 1975
—, *The Duchess of Malfi*, New Mermaids, 1987
—, *The White Devil*, New Mermaids, 1966

John Russell Brown (ed.), *The Duchess of Malfi*, Revels Student Editions, 1997
—, *The White Devil*, Revels Student editions, 1996

Kay W. David (ed.), John Marston, *The Malcontent* with additions by John Webster, New Mermaids, 1998

Jonathan Dollimore and Alan Sinfield (eds.), *Selected Plays of John Webster*, Cambridge University Press, 1983

Richard Dutton (ed.), *Monuments of Honour* in *Jacobean City Pageants*, Keele University Press, 1995

David Gunby, David Carnegie, MacDonald P. Jackson (eds.), *Appius and Virginia: a Tragedy* (1655) in volume 2 of *The Works of John Webster* (an old-spelling critical edition), Cambridge UP, 1995–2007

Arthur Kinney (ed.), *The Witch of Edmonton* by Dekker, Ford & Rowley (and possibly Webster), New Mermaids, 1998

F. L. Lucas (ed.), *The Complete Works of John Webster*, 4 volumes, Chatto and Windus, first published 1927, reprinted 1966

John Webster, *Northwood Ho* (1607), written with Thomas Dekker, *Old English Drama*: 91, facsimile edition, Amersham, issued for subscribers by John S. Farmer

René Weis (ed.), *A Cure for a Cuckold, The Devil's Lawcase, The Duchess of Malfi, The White Devil*, Oxford World Classics, 1996

A Monumental Column: Funeral elegy on the death of Henry Prince of Wales is freely available at: **http://www.uoregon.edu**

GOTHIC TEXTS

Charlotte Brontë, *Jane Eyre*, 1847

Angela Carter, *The Bloody Chamber*, 1979

Geoffrey Chaucer, *The Pardoner's Tale*, c. 1390

Charles Dickens, *The Mystery of Edwin Drood*, 1870

John Milton, *Paradise Lost*, 1667

Ann Radcliffe, *The Mysteries of Udolpho*, 1794

William Shakespeare, *Macbeth*, 1603

Mary Shelley, *Frankenstein*, 1818

Bram Stoker, *Dracula*, 1897

LITERARY AND SOCIAL BACKGROUND

Fredson Bower, *Elizabethan Revenge Tragedy 1587–1642*, P. Smith, 1959
  Standard discussion of genre, useful on social background to plays

Nicholas Brooke, *Horrid Laughter in Jacobean Tragedy*, Open Books, 1979
  Focus on black humour in plays

Jonathan Culler, *Literary Theory: A Very Short Introduction*, Oxford UP, 1997
  A very short, accessible and comprehensive introduction to a complex subject

Andrew Gurr, *The Shakespearean Stage 1574–1642*, Cambridge UP, 1992
  Indispensable guide to the theatre of the period

Ann Rosalind Jones, 'Italians and Others: *The White Devil* (1612)' in *Staging the Renaissance*, edited by Kastan and Stallybrass, Routledge, 1991, pages 251–62
  Useful discussion of contemporary ideas about Italy

David Scott Kastan and Peter Stallybrass (eds.), *Staging the Renaissance: Reinterpretations of Elizabethan and Jacobean Drama*, Routledge, 1991
  Excellent collection of articles on all aspects of drama, includes Jones's discussion of Italy in relation to *The White Devil*

FURTHER READING

Alexander Leggatt, *English Drama: Shakespeare to the Restoration, 1590 –1660*, Longman, 1988
   Standard guide to drama of period with short biographies and discussions of most important works

David McLellan (ed.), *Karl Marx: Selected Writings*, Oxford UP, 1977
   Careful selection of most important writings

R. W. Maslen, *Elizabethan Fictions: Espionage, Counter-espionage and the Duplicity of Fiction in Early Elizabethan Prose Narratives*, Clarendon Press, 1997
   Examines the relationship between writing and spying and the dubious reputation enjoyed by writers

Lawrence Stone, *The Family, Sex and Marriage in England 1500–1800*, Penguin Books, 1977
   Well-researched overview of sexual mores and changing forms of marriage

LITERARY CRITICISM

Kate Aughterson, *Webster: The Tragedies*, Palgrave, 2001
   Useful account of *The White Devil* and *The Duchess of Malfi* with detailed discussion of individual scenes and Webster's dramaturgy

Catherine Belsey, *The Subject of Tragedy: Identity & Difference in Renaissance Drama*, Methuen, 1985
   Seminal study of changing ideas about identity charted through **tragedies**

Ralph Berry, *The Art of John Webster*, Clarendon Press: Oxford, 1972
   Well-written and with a great deal of insight, a thoughtful, detailed and convincing account

Travis Bogard, *The Tragic Satire of John Webster*, Russell and Russell, 1965
   Examines complex mixture of styles employed by Webster, especially his uncomfortable combination of tragedy and **satire**

M. C. Bradbrook, *John Webster Citizen and Dramatist*, Weidenfeld and Nicolson, 1980
   Biographical account of Webster and his social milieu including interesting chapters on other significant characters such as Penelope Devereux

Richard Allen Cave, *Text & Performance: The White Devil and The Duchess of Malfi*, Macmillan, 1988
   Good overview of performances up to late 1980s

Anders Dallby, *The Anatomy of Evil: A Study of John Webster's The White Devil*, CWK Gleerup Lund, 1974
> Good overview of earlier critics' conflicting reactions to play which attempts to analyse the play's unique qualities

Jonathan Dollimore, *Radical Tragedy*, Harvester Wheatsheaf, 1984
> Idiosyncratic and thought-provoking overview of plays in period

Charles R. Forker, *Skull Beneath the Skin: The Achievement of John Webster*, Southern Illinois UP, 1986
> Solid, detailed biography of Webster with useful discussion of writing

Dena Goldberg, *Between Worlds: A Study of the Plays of John Webster*, Wilfrid Laurier UP, 1987
> Socio-political account of Webster's plays in context of early modern culture

G. K. and S. K. Hunter (eds.), *John Webster: A Critical Anthology*, Penguin Books, 1969
> Useful anthology of writing about Webster up to late 1960s

Clifford Leech, *John Webster: A Critical Study*, Haskell House, 1970
> Some interesting observations about plays and Webster's writing but has been superseded by more recent accounts

Christina Luckyj, *A Winter's Snake: Dramatic Form in the Tragedies of John Webster*, University of Georgia Press, 1989
> Mainly focused on discussion of plots/sub-plots

Kathleen McLuskie, *Renaissance Dramatists: Feminist Reading*, Harvester Wheatsheaf, 1989
> Useful overview and sophisticated discussion of feminist accounts

Brian Morris (ed.), *Mermaid Critical Commentaries: John Webster*, Ernest Benn, 1970
> Collection of critical writings on Webster up to late 1960s

Jacqueline Pearson, *Tragedy and tragicomedy in the plays of John Webster*, Manchester UP, 1980
> Examines mixture of elements in plays, arguing that Webster combines tragedy with tragicomedy

Rowland Wymer, *Webster & Ford*, St Martin's Press, 1995
> Useful overview of dramatists, includes a chapter on *The White Devil*

LITERARY TERMS

allusion a passing reference in a work of literature to something outside the text; may include other works of literature, myth, historical facts or biographical detail

ambiguity the capacity of words and sentences to have double, multiple or uncertain meanings; a structural feature of Webster's play

aside when a character speaks in such a way that some or all of the other characters on stage cannot hear what is being said; or they address the audience directly. It is a device used to reveal a character's private thoughts, emotions and intentions

comedy originally a play with a happy ending; later the term was used for a humorous or funny play

couplet a pair of rhymed lines in any metre

courtly love medieval conception of love as noble, courteous and pure, concerned with a knight serving a lady and performing brave deeds to win her love. Since it was not based on marriage the love was also adulterous

dramatic irony when the implications of an episode or a speech are better understood by the audience than the characters

dumb show action presented on stage without words; common in medieval and Renaissance drama

epic lengthy narrative poem relating heroic deeds, for example Homer's *Iliad* and *Odyssey*, or Virgil's *Aeneid*

gothic a literary genre (originally associated with the eighteenth century) which combined horror and romance and featured supernatural elements such as ghosts, madness, haunted houses, secrets, and castles with winding passages

imagery descriptive language which uses images to make actions, objects and characters more vivid in the reader's mind. Metaphors and similes are examples of imagery

iambic pentameter a line of poetry consisting of five iambic feet (iambic consisting of a weak syllable followed by a strong one)

irony the humorous or sarcastic use of words to imply the opposite of what they normally mean; incongruity between what might be expected and what actually happens; the ill-timed arrival of an event that had been hoped for

malcontent a character discontented with their lot in life who rails against society; common in Renaissance drama

melodrama a form of drama in which extravagant and sensational deeds and thinly-drawn characters occur, with strong elements of violence, sexuality and evil and a simplistic moral or judicial code

metadrama, metatheatre drama which draws attention to its own fictionality and use of dramatic devices, for example by direct address to the audience, references to its status as play or techniques such as a 'play-within-a-play'

metaphor a figure of speech in which a word or phrase is applied to an object, a character or an action which does not literally belong to it, in order to imply a resemblance and create an unusual or striking image in the reader's mind

metonym figure of speech characterised by substituting a word or phrase which constitutes part of a whole for the whole; the adjective derived from this practice is 'metonymically'

metre the rhythmic arrangement of syllables in poetic verse

paradox a seemingly absurd or self-contradictory statement

parody an imitation of a work of literature, literary style or cultural practice designed to ridicule the original

patriarchy system of social organisation in which men predominate in positions of power and influence, often over and at the expense of women who are subservient

personification literary usage which turns inanimate objects or abstract qualities into people

quatrain a four line stanza in poetry

revenge drama/tragedy dramatic genre popular in the late-sixteenth and early-seventeenth century in which the main protagonist is determined to avenge a crime which is beyond the reach of normal justice, often due to the criminal's elevated social position

satire a type of literature in which folly, evil or topical issues are held up to scorn through ridicule, **irony** or exaggeration; the adjective derived from this is 'satirical'

simile a figure of speech which compares two things using the words 'like' or 'as'

soliloquy a dramatic device which allows a character to speak directly to the audience as if thinking aloud, revealing their inner thoughts, feelings and intentions

subtext an underlying or hidden theme in a piece of writing

tragedy in its original sense, a drama dealing with elevated actions and emotions and characters of high social standing in which a terrible outcome becomes inevitable as a result of an unstoppable sequence of events and a fatal flaw in the personality of the protagonist. More recently, tragedy has come to include courses of events happening to ordinary individuals that are inevitable because of social and cultural conditions and natural disasters

tragicomedy a play combining the qualities of a **tragedy** and a **comedy**, or containing both tragic and comic elements; sometimes a play mainly of tragic character, but with a happy ending

THE AUTHOR OF THESE NOTES

Jan Sewell studied for a degree in English and Hispanic Studies and a master's degree in Cultural Studies at the University of Birmingham before completing her PhD at the Shakespeare Institute, Stratford-upon-Avon. She has taught at the Universities of Birmingham and Wolverhampton and the Shakespeare Institute. She currently teaches at the University of Warwick and the Open University. She was Associate Editor of the *RSC Complete Works of Shakespeare* and has published work on Renaissance and Spanish Golden Age Drama.

GCSE

Maya Angelou
I Know Why the Caged Bird Sings

Jane Austen
Pride and Prejudice

Alan Ayckbourn
Absent Friends

Elizabeth Barrett Browning
Selected Poems

Robert Bolt
A Man for All Seasons

Harold Brighouse
Hobson's Choice

Charlotte Brontë
Jane Eyre

Emily Brontë
Wuthering Heights

Brian Clark
Whose Life is it Anyway?

Robert Cormier
Heroes

Shelagh Delaney
A Taste of Honey

Charles Dickens
David Copperfield
Great Expectations
Hard Times
Oliver Twist
Selected Stories

Roddy Doyle
Paddy Clarke Ha Ha Ha

George Eliot
Silas Marner
The Mill on the Floss

Anne Frank
The Diary of a Young Girl

William Golding
Lord of the Flies

Oliver Goldsmith
She Stoops to Conquer

Willis Hall
The Long and the Short and the Tall

Thomas Hardy
Far from the Madding Crowd
The Mayor of Casterbridge
Tess of the d'Urbervilles
The Withered Arm and other Wessex Tales

L. P. Hartley
The Go-Between

Seamus Heaney
Selected Poems

Susan Hill
I'm the King of the Castle

Barry Hines
A Kestrel for a Knave

Louise Lawrence
Children of the Dust

Harper Lee
To Kill a Mockingbird

Laurie Lee
Cider with Rosie

Arthur Miller
The Crucible
A View from the Bridge

Robert O'Brien
Z for Zachariah

Frank O'Connor
My Oedipus Complex and Other Stories

George Orwell
Animal Farm

J.B. Priestley
An Inspector Calls
When We Are Married

Willy Russell
Educating Rita
Our Day Out

J. D. Salinger
The Catcher in the Rye

William Shakespeare
Henry IV Part I
Henry V
Julius Caesar
Macbeth
The Merchant of Venice
A Midsummer Night's Dream
Much Ado About Nothing
Romeo and Juliet
The Tempest
Twelfth Night

George Bernard Shaw
Pygmalion

Mary Shelley
Frankenstein

R.C. Sherriff
Journey's End

Rukshana Smith
Salt on the snow

John Steinbeck
Of Mice and Men

Robert Louis Stevenson
Dr Jekyll and Mr Hyde

Jonathan Swift
Gulliver's Travels

Robert Swindells
Daz 4 Zoe

Mildred D. Taylor
Roll of Thunder, Hear My Cry

Mark Twain
Huckleberry Finn

James Watson
Talking in Whispers

Edith Wharton
Ethan Frome

William Wordsworth
Selected Poems

A Choice of Poets

Mystery Stories of the Nineteenth Century including The Signalman

Nineteenth Century Short Stories

Poetry of the First World War

Six Women Poets

For the AQA Anthology:

Duffy and Armitage & Pre-1914 Poetry

Heaney and Clarke & Pre-1914 Poetry

Poems from Different Cultures

Key Stage 3

William Shakespeare
Henry V
Macbeth
Much Ado About Nothing
Richard III
The Tempest

Margaret Atwood
Cat's Eye
The Handmaid's Tale

Jane Austen
Emma
Mansfield Park
Persuasion
Pride and Prejudice
Sense and Sensibility

William Blake
Songs of Innocence and of Experience

The Brontës
Selected Poems

Charlotte Brontë
Jane Eyre
Villette

Emily Brontë
Wuthering Heights

Angela Carter
The Bloody Chamber
Nights at the Circus
Wise Children

Geoffrey Chaucer
The Franklin's Prologue and Tale
The Merchant's Prologue and Tale
The Miller's Prologue and Tale
The Pardoner's Tale
The Prologue to the Canterbury Tales
The Wife of Bath's Prologue and Tale

Caryl Churchill
Top Girls

John Clare
Selected Poems

Joseph Conrad
Heart of Darkness

Charles Dickens
Bleak House
Great Expectations
Hard Times

Emily Dickinson
Selected Poems

Carol Ann Duffy
Selected Poems
The World's Wife

George Eliot
Middlemarch
The Mill on the Floss

T. S. Eliot
Selected Poems
The Waste Land

F. Scott Fitzgerald
The Great Gatsby

John Ford
'Tis Pity She's a Whore

Michael Frayn
Spies

Charles Frazier
Cold Mountain

Brian Friel
Making History
Translations

William Golding
The Spire

Thomas Hardy
Jude the Obscure
The Mayor of Casterbridge
The Return of the Native
Selected Poems
Tess of the d'Urbervilles

Seamus Heaney
Selected Poems from 'Opened Ground'

Nathaniel Hawthorne
The Scarlet Letter

Homer
The Iliad
The Odyssey

Aldous Huxley
Brave New World

Henrik Ibsen
A Doll's House

Kazuo Ishiguro
The Remains of the Day

James Joyce
Dubliners

John Keats
Selected Poems

Philip Larkin
High Windows
The Whitsun Weddings and Selected Poems

Ian McEwan
Atonement

Christopher Marlowe
Doctor Faustus
Edward II

Arthur Miller
All My Sons
Death of a Salesman

John Milton
Paradise Lost Books I & II

Toni Morrison
Beloved

George Orwell
Nineteen Eighty-Four

Sylvia Plath
Selected Poems

William Shakespeare
Antony and Cleopatra
As You Like It
Hamlet
Henry IV Part I
King Lear
Macbeth
Measure for Measure
The Merchant of Venice
A Midsummer Night's Dream
Much Ado About Nothing
Othello
Richard II
Richard III
Romeo and Juliet
The Taming of the Shrew
The Tempest
Twelfth Night
The Winter's Tale

Mary Shelley
Frankenstein

Richard Brinsley Sheridan
The School for Scandal

Bram Stoker
Dracula

Alfred Tennyson
Selected Poems

Alice Walker
The Color Purple

John Webster
The Duchess of Malfi
The White Devil

Oscar Wilde
The Importance of Being Earnest
A Woman of No Importance

Tennessee Williams
Cat on a Hot Tin Roof
The Glass Menagerie
A Streetcar Named Desire

Jeanette Winterson
Oranges Are Not the Only Fruit

Virginia Woolf
To the Lighthouse

William Wordsworth
The Prelude and Selected Poems

W. B. Yeats
Selected Poems

Poetry of the First World War